End

Invitations to ~~Discipleship~~

Morna D. Hooker

First published jointly in 2003, in the United States by
Hendrickson Publishers, and in Great Britain by SCM Press,
9–17 St Albans Place, London N1 0NX

ISBN 1-56563-356-3

Hendrickson Edition First Printing – September 2003

Hendrickson Publishers' edition published by arrangement with
SCM Press, a division of SCM-Canterbury Press Ltd.

Typeset by Regent Typesetting, London
Printed in Great Britain by Creative Print and Design, Wales

To my colleagues
in the Cambridge University Faculty of Divinity
in appreciation

We shall not cease from exploration
And the end of all our exploring
Will be to arrive where we started
And know the place for the first time.

(T.S. Eliot, *Four Quartets*, Little Gidding V)

Contents

Preface

This book had its origins in a Valedictory Lecture given in the University of Cambridge in the summer of 1998, on my retirement from the Lady Margaret's chair of Divinity. Having failed, 22 years previously, to respond to the University's invitation to deliver an Inaugural Lecture, it seemed appropriate to explore a theme which linked Endings with Beginnings.[1] That Valedictory Lecture also provided the occasion to celebrate the successful completion of a fundraising exercise which meant that the Faculty of Divinity would be able to move from the old 'Divinity School' to a new building: the end of one phase of the Faculty's life was about to give way to the beginning of a new one. It is to my colleagues in the Faculty over those 22 years, in recognition of their friendship, that I dedicate this book.

The original lecture has formed the basis of lectures to various Theological Societies in recent years. Most recently, in February 2003, I lectured on the same theme at Fuller Theological Seminary. I am grateful to Professor Donald Hagner for the invitation to lecture there, and for the warm hospitality extended to me by Don and his wife Beverley during my stay in Pasadena.

The expansion of the original lecture into a book was

vii

suggested by the Revd Dr John Bowden, who was editor of the SCM Press at the time of its delivery. An invitation from Professor Lung-kwong Lo to give the Chuen King Lectures in Hong Kong in 2001 provided the opportunity to begin the process of expansion. It was a great privilege to be asked to deliver these lectures, and I would like to express again my gratitude to Professor Lo and his colleagues – in particular to Dr Eric Wong – for their hospitality, and for the warm welcome they gave me to Chung Chi College in the Chinese University of Hong Kong. The constraints of that lectureship – three lectures only, and rather shorter than usual because of the need to translate the lectures into Chinese as they were delivered – means that the final form of the book is considerably longer than the lectures. I hope, nevertheless, that my many friends in Hong Kong will recognize some of the things said in these chapters.

Finally, I would like to express my thanks to the Revd Dr Anthony Bash for once again casting a careful eye over the drafts of my chapters, and for encouraging me to continue with the task of writing this book.

M.D.H.

The publisher would like to thank Faber and Faber Ltd for permission to quote from *Collected Poems 1909–1962*, by T.S. Eliot.

Beginnings and Endings

The beginning shall remind us of the end.

(T.S. Eliot, *The Cultivation of Christmas Trees*)

Beginning a new enterprise is always difficult, for one is naturally anxious to make a good impression. Beginning any *literary* work – whether a lecture, novel, essay or sermon – is a challenge: one needs to catch the attention of listeners or readers and make them want to hear or read more. Beginnings are important – and they were especially so in the ancient world, where the vast proportion of the population relied on the spoken rather than the written word. Books were written to be read aloud, and it was therefore important to give essential information at the beginning of a book, for listeners could not thumb back through the pages – or unroll the scroll – looking for something they had missed. It was important, too, for authors to give some indication as to what kind of book one was writing, for there were no glossy covers with publishers' blurbs on the back, to put potential readers or listeners in the picture. Essential clues had to be there in the opening paragraphs of the book.

There are certain literary conventions about how to begin. Traditional fairy-stories always begin, 'Once upon a time . . .'. Hearing those four words, one knows immediately what kind of story to expect. Our letters begin 'Dear so-and-so'. Greek dramas began with 'prologues', which provided the audience with the information they needed to understand the story they were about to see played out on the stage. This information was not simply about the place and time of the action, the identity of the characters and who was related to whom, but concerned the deeper significance of the story: the playwright invited his audience to share his insights into the unseen forces – perhaps the just demands of the gods, or perhaps simply their caprice – that were at work in the events which he portrayed on the stage.

Endings are equally important. Taking leave of something or someone is often difficult. And so is concluding a literary work. Once you have set something in motion, it is important to know how to come to a stop – you cannot simply jump out of a moving vehicle. Sometimes, of course, speakers do not seem to know *how* to stop – rather like those planes coming into land at a busy airport, which circle round and round, waiting for an opportunity to land. Again, there are certain literary conventions: letters will end with some established formula, such as 'Yours sincerely', or 'Yours faithfully', after-dinner jokes will end with a punch line, addresses at an evangelistic rally will end with an appeal. The traditional fairy-story ends, 'And they lived happily ever after', and one knows that the story has been rounded off satisfactorily. Modern novels, to be sure, often seem to end in mid-air, leaving one wondering, 'But what happened next?' But preachers who end a sermon without some kind of challenge may leave their congregations wondering what they have been trying to say. Whether writing or speaking, it is important to provide one's hearers or readers with something memorable to take away, either in the form of pleasure at a story that has come to a neat conclusion, or in the form of a challenge to think and act.

There are obvious similarities, then, between literary beginnings and endings. There are, however, more important links. It is not simply that these are the two most difficult parts of any enterprise to get right, though that is true, since, as with travelling by air, it is always take-off and landing that are the two most dangerous moments. There is also frequently a literary and thematic connection between the beginning and the end of a composition. Tidy endings often take us back to where we began: a skilful use of what the literary critics call *inclusio* reminds us that it was, after all, the writer's purpose all along to lead us to precisely this point. This return to beginnings is, moreover, a biblical theme. The lost paradise of Genesis 1 becomes the blueprint for paradise restored; the eschatological hope, set out by the Hebrew prophets and by Jewish writers of the Second Temple period, is that the end of time will correspond to the beginning. When men and women obey God's will, and once again see him face to face and reflect his glory, then creation itself will be restored. The end which brings us back to the beginning forms a satisfying conclusion. In recent years, I have found astrophysicists presenting a negative version of the same idea, for they tell us that the universe which began the size of a pea will finally collapse into a black hole of similar dimensions.

When, many centuries ago, the Greek philosopher Heraclitus declared beginning and end to be common, he was apparently thinking of a circle,[1] and literary critics tend to describe this return to base in a narrative as circularity. Yet the relationship between beginning and end is more complex than that. The end of the biblical narrative does not *simply* take us back to where we began, for it has a story to tell and a journey to make. The Garden of Eden portrayed in Genesis and the heavenly Jerusalem described in the Revelation of St John are not, after all, identical, though they may share certain features. If at the end of the story we return to the beginning, we nevertheless see things in a new light.

This correspondence of beginnings and endings is a feature of a great deal of literature, both ancient and modern. It is found in many of our New Testament documents, and it is this theme that I want to explore, looking at those books that have a story to tell, namely the Gospels and Acts, where it is most clearly evident.[2] We shall discover that their beginnings and ends not only belong together but also point forward and backward to the significance of the story that lies in-between; more than that, the beginnings point backward and the ends point forward to what lies *beyond* the narrative, reminding us that the story they enclose is but a part of a longer, ongoing story. I shall mention the beginnings only in passing, since I have already attempted to explore that theme in an earlier book, in which I tried to show how the introduction to each Gospel serves as a key to help us to understand the rest of what each evangelist has written.[3] But because beginnings and endings are related, the beginnings cannot be ignored.

The Gospels' introductions give us clues about their content. If the Gospels were detective stories, one would say that in each of their introductions the individual author had given us the solution to the plot before beginning his tale. Now Gospels are plainly *not* detective stories, but what they *are* it is far more difficult to say. For centuries they were treated as biographies, a view which was thrown out when it was realized that their traditional title, 'Gospel', meaning 'good news', was far more appropriate; they are in fact propaganda, the story of Jesus told with a very particular purpose. Recent attempts to reinstate the Gospels as biographies[4] seem to me to be unpersuasive, and one notable difference between the Gospels and ancient biographies is that the Gospels do not *end* like biographies. The normal biography ends with the death of the great man and an assessment of his achievements – perhaps a eulogy or an account of public reaction to his death;[5] that is not how our Gospels end.

The Gospels perhaps have more in common with certain Jewish books which focus on the life of a particular man or woman: in our 'Old Testament', for example, we find the stories of Ruth and Esther, and – though greatly expanded by theological discourse – the story of Job; in extra-canonical literature, we have the stories of Judith and of Joseph and Asenath. These stories mostly conform to the true fairy-tale format – in the book of Ruth quite literally, for Ruth and Boaz marry and may be presumed to live 'happily ever after', as also may Joseph and Asenath. As for Judith and Esther, they both triumph over the nation's enemies, while Job, who lost his seven sons and three daughters and all his animals at the beginning of the narrative, is provided with another seven sons and three daughters to replace those he lost, and twice as many sheep and camels, oxen and donkeys as he had before. The storyteller has wrapped the whole thing up neatly – perhaps a little *too* neatly, for though Job seems satisfied, one is left a little uneasy by the way his ten children are so easily replaced by ten more. Many commentators are puzzled: they feel that a 'happy ending' conflicts with the rest of the book, which has *resisted* the conventional belief that the righteous are always rewarded and the wicked punished. But the prose sections at the beginning and end of the book form an *inclusio*, and these final verses remind us of the opening chapters of the book, even if we do not return to the scene of the heavenly court. The restoration of Job's fortunes is the indication that he has passed the test, and that Satan has failed.

A rather different ending is found in the book of Jonah; here, to be sure, everything ends happily for the inhabitants of Nineveh, but Jonah himself is left, at the end of the story, sulking by the side of his withered castor-oil bush; remarkably, this book ends with God asking a question: 'Should I not be concerned about Nineveh, that great city, in which there are more than a hundred and twenty thousand persons who do not know their right hand from their left, and also many animals?' We turn the page, expecting an answer, but there is none. Was Jonah silenced? What did he do next? Did he catch the next boat home? Was that really the end of the story? Does this book not undermine all our assumptions about the importance of having a satisfactory ending?

Now the interesting thing about *all* these stories – even the story of Ruth and Boaz, with its 'fairy-story' ending – is that each of them has a moral; they are all told with apologetic purpose. When we probe the meaning of these stories, we realize that this apologetic purpose dictates the ending. Normally, of course, this is a 'happy ending' showing how faith in God triumphs. But these are not just good yarns, intended to entertain their hearers and to send them home at the end of the evening feeling that they have been well entertained – they are intended, like Jesus' parables, to make their hearers think. Nowhere, however, is that clearer than in Jonah, and that is partly due to the way in which the story has been told. Instead of the tidy ending which leaves everything sorted out, and gives us a sense of a story well told, we have the untidy, open-ended conclusion which leaves us dissatisfied, wondering what happened next – and even more importantly, wondering what it means *for us*. For when a story stops rather than coming to a conclusion, we feel involved: we want to step into the plot and sort things out. We may well feel that we want to round the story off by throwing Jonah back into the sea; but we may also find ourselves wondering, 'Does this really mean, then, that God cares about those awful Ninevites?' The end of the story is, as it were, suspended, waiting for *us* to finish it off.[6]

We might well expect the so-called 'historical' books of the Old Testament to end in a more conclusive fashion, but surprisingly this is not so. Genesis ends, to be sure, with the death of Joseph, but his last words are an assurance to his people that God will bring them into the land that he promised to Abraham, Isaac and Jacob, and that they will carry his bones with them (Gen. 50.24–6): death in Egypt is clearly not the end of the story. Exodus concludes with a description of how Moses used to set up the tabernacle, and how the cloud would cover it – an indication that God's glory was filling it: when the cloud moved, so did the people (Exodus 40). The book ends, then, with Israel on the move: the story is to be continued. Both Leviticus and Numbers end with the statement that 'These are the commandments which God gave to/through Moses' – in Leviticus on Sinai, in Numbers in the lowlands of Moab; in neither book has Israel yet entered the Promised Land. The final scene in Deuteronomy shows us Moses climbing Mount Pisgah and looking out over the Promised Land (chapter 34). There he dies, after hearing God repeat the promise to give it to Abraham's descendants. Once again, we know that there is more to come, even though we have now come to the end of the Pentateuch – that is, to the end of the five books that were traditionally attributed to Moses.

The book of Joshua appears to be a more complete story, beginning with an account of how Joshua was commanded by God to take over from Moses (1.1–9), and ending with Joshua's death and the burial of Joseph's bones (24.29–33). But Judges ends with the comment that 'in those days there was no king in Israel; all the people did what was right in their own eyes' (21.25). Clearly we are being invited to think forward, to the time when there *would* be kings. 1–2 Samuel and 1–2 Kings really form one account:[7] the last part, 2 Kings, ends with Jehoiachin of Judah being released from prison, but still in exile. The people's hopes of returning to their own land are still unfulfilled. 1–2 Chronicles also belong together, and in the last chapter of 2 Chronicles we are told of the destruction of the temple and the exile of the people. Then, in a final paragraph, we read how, after

70 years, the Persian king, Cyrus, decreed that God had commanded him to rebuild the temple, and how he summoned the people to return (2 Chron. 36.22–3). These are the final words in what was to become the last book in the Hebrew Bible! It could hardly have had a more 'open' ending.[8]

The Song of Solomon, a collection of love poems, is full of expectation, and ends with an appeal to the writer's beloved to 'make haste' (8.14). The prophetic books are equally open-ended. Jeremiah ends, like 2 Kings and 2 Chronicles, with Jehoiachin of Judah in exile. Almost all the rest end with passages that look forward to what is going to happen: God is going to make 'new heavens' and a 'new earth' (Isa. 66.22), and 'plant' his people in the land he has given them (Amos 9.11–15). He will have compassion on his people and forgive them (Mic. 7.18–20) and bring them back from exile (Zeph. 3.16–20). He will overthrow kingdoms and establish his servant Zerubbabel (Hag. 2.20–3) and make Jerusalem holy (Zech. 14.20–1). He will send the prophet Elijah before him (Mal. 4.5–6), and when he comes, he will dwell in Zion (Joel 3.21). Hosea ends with an appeal to the people to return to God (Hos. 14.1–9), and Obadiah with a promise that the exiles will be brought home (Obad. vv. 20–1). In Lamentations, we have an appeal to God to restore his people (Lam. 5.19–22), while Daniel ends with a calculation of the number of years 'until the time of the end' (Dan. 12.9). Habakkuk expresses his trust in God, even while waiting for the day of calamity (Hab. 3.16–19). Only Nahum ends in what is apparently total despair (chapter 3).

No doubt this 'open-endedness' is largely due to the fact

that the compilers of the prophetic books tended to round them off with oracles that expressed hope in God's coming salvation. The result, however, is that almost all our Old Testament books have conclusions that look forward to what is going to happen next. We shall not be surprised, then, if we find that the Gospels do the same – for though they announce that God's salvation has now come, in the person of Jesus, they still look forward to the future consummation of all things.[9]

Our concern, as we explore the final pages of each Gospel and of Acts, will not be with *historical* issues – with what precisely happened, and whether or not the accounts of resurrection appearances can be reconciled. Nor will it be to attempt to trace how the traditions developed or to see whether we can discern earlier traditions behind these books. Our aim is simply to examine how the evangelists handled the material, and to uncover the message that they hoped to convey to their readers.

2

Mark's Ending: Lost or Suspended?

. . . the end precedes the beginning,
And the end and the beginning were always there
Before the beginning and after the end.

(T.S. Eliot, *Four Quartets*, Burnt Norton V)

When we turn to our Gospels, we do indeed discover that they, too, all conclude with suspended endings, leaving us uneasy, dissatisfied, wondering what happens next. Nowhere is that clearer than in the case of Mark. In chapter 15, he has told the story of Jesus' crucifixion, death and burial, and now, in chapter 16, he concludes his Gospel with one short paragraph. After a brief account of how some women came to Jesus' tomb, found it empty, and were told by a strange young man that Jesus had been raised and that his disciples were to go to Galilee, Mark's story comes to an abrupt conclusion at 16.8: 'and the women said nothing to anyone, for they were afraid'. We feel outraged: the story is only half-told. Our questions are all unanswered: Who had rolled away the stone from the tomb? Who was the mysterious young man in white? Was his message that Jesus had been raised from the dead true? Did the disciples go to Galilee and see him? And how did they ever receive the message if the women were too frightened to pass on the news?

But when we turn the page in our modern Bibles, we do not find a blank, as with Jonah, but two attempts to conclude Mark's story. These are printed as two brief paragraphs at the end of the Gospel in our Bibles, but they are certainly spurious, for their style and vocabulary are clearly at variance with Mark's own.[1] It is hardly surprising if various scribes attempted at a very early stage to round the story off, for his ending seems extraordinarily abrupt. Nor is it surprising if, for centuries, scholars assumed that the end of Mark's Gospel must be missing. How *could* he leave his readers with all these unanswered questions? His ending seemed unsatisfactory from a literary point of view, since we are left wondering what happened next; it also seemed unsatisfactory grammatically, for his final word was the conjunction *gar*, meaning 'for', and finding this at the end of a sentence was regarded as the equivalent of ending an English sentence with a preposition; worst of all, it seemed unsatisfactory theologically. For if Mark's Gospel ends at verse 8, then we are left without witnesses to the resurrection: all we have is a tomb which had been broken open and which was said by some unidentified witness to be empty, together with a message that Jesus had been raised from the dead which was entrusted to some women. The message was neither substantiated nor passed on, but even if the women *had* reported what had happened, their words would have been regarded as worthless, since Jewish law demanded the evidence of two *male* witnesses to establish the truth. How *could* Mark end his story here, with the statement that the women were terrified as his final words?

Mark's Ending: Lost or Suspended?

If he did end here, then the final words of his Gospel – his presentation of the 'Good News' – were words of human failure, incomprehension, disobedience and fear.

The theory that the ending of Mark has been lost is equally difficult, however; one might perhaps lose the last page of a codex – but how could one lose the end of a scroll? Did it perhaps tear off with too much use? If that happened, the ending would be well-known and remembered, and could easily be replaced. Was the scroll set aside and neglected, and the end perhaps chewed by vermin? In that case, as one scholar put it, if mice nibbled the last page, they were remarkably discerning mice to stop just where they did![2] So if the ending was not in fact lost, was the Gospel perhaps never completed? Was Mark prevented by some unhappy circumstance from completing his Gospel? Might he even have been martyred, while still penning the final paragraphs? It would certainly have been appropriate if the evangelist who insisted so vehemently that those who followed Jesus must be prepared to take up the cross and follow him to death was himself martyred, but tradition is silent on this point.

There is, however, a third possibility. Could it be that the Gospel ends where Mark intended it to end? Recent commentators on Mark have come to believe that Mark's abrupt ending was deliberate.[3] He has been found to be in good literary company,[4] for though Aristotle insisted that 'well-constructed plots should neither begin nor end at an arbitrary point',[5] Homer's *Iliad* stops almost as abruptly as Mark, with various key expectations still unfulfilled,[6] and the ending of the *Odyssey* is thought by many to have been written later than the rest of the book.[7] Mark's grammatical crime turns out to be not as great as was once thought, for parallels to his final *gar* have been found elsewhere;[8] moreover, his whole book is characterized by a rough Greek style. Theologically, too, Mark's ending is entirely in character with the rest of his book. His very last phrase, 'they were afraid' (*ephobounto gar*), echoes many earlier statements, for throughout his story Mark has emphasized the fear and incomprehension with which people reacted to Jesus. Now, at the end of the story, the women are confronted by news of the most powerful act of all, and it is hardly surprising if they are afraid.

Among the examples of sentences ending with *gar* that have been discovered there are two striking parallels to Mark 16.8 in the Septuagint, the Greek translation of the Old Testament, which was probably the version known to Mark. In Genesis 18.15 we read how Sarah, who had laughed when she had overheard Abraham being told that she would bear a son, denied that she had laughed, 'for she was afraid' (*ephobēthē gar*). The explanation of her fear has already been given in verses 13–14: 'Why did Sarah laugh and say, "Shall I, being old, really bear a child?" Is anything impossible with God?' Clearly the reason for Sarah's fear – like that of the women at the tomb – is the astonishing and overwhelming creative power of God, in which she is unable to believe. Could Mark have had this in mind? If so, there is an intriguing link with the argument in Romans 4, where Paul describes Abraham's reaction to God's promise to give him a son, and identifies Abraham's faith in 'the God who gives life to the dead and calls things that do not exist into existence' (v. 17) with the faith of Christians in the resurrection (vv. 19–25). God's announcement can be met with fear (as by Sarah and by the women) or by faith (as by Abraham and by Christians, who believe that Christ has been raised). The second example is found in Genesis 45.3, where Joseph discloses his identity to his brothers, who had believed him to be dead, and they are unable to answer him, 'for they were thrown into confusion' (*etarachthēsan gar*).⁹ Once again, we have people overcome with fear, and here, too, the announcement of the news that someone is alive leads to their silence: its hearers are incapable of grasping it. Although the echoes of these passages in Mark 16.8 are almost certainly accidental, it would nevertheless seem that this construction with *gar* was an entirely natural – and appropriate – one for Mark to use.

Mark describes the reaction of the women to what they see and hear in vivid detail. He tells us that they were greatly alarmed (*exethambēthēsan*) when they entered the tomb and saw the young man (v. 5).¹⁰ When they heard the young man's message they fled from the tomb because they had been overcome by trembling and terror (v. 8a). The word 'terror' (*ekstasis*) is found elsewhere in Mark only in 5.42, where it is used, together with its cognate verb, to describe the disciples' reaction to a young girl's resurrection; in the same narrative, the woman with a haemorrhage, knowing that she has been healed, is described as 'fearful and trembling' (*phobētheisa kai tremousa*, v. 33) when she makes herself known to Jesus. Alarm, terror and trembling are the natural human reactions to the power of God.¹¹ It is hardly surprising if the women react in this way to the news of Jesus' resurrection.

Mark's final words, however, describe the women's fear,

and this word has far more negative connotations. Those who have faith in God should not fear.[12] Earlier in his story, Mark had described how, when Jairus was brought news of his daughter's death, Jesus had said to him, 'Do not fear; only believe' (5.36). Now, at the tomb of someone they presume to be dead, the women fear because they do not believe. Again and again throughout his ministry, Jesus has met with lack of faith. Remarkably, those who *have* shown faith have been women, who have been praised because of it;[13] and now it seems that even the women fail, for they cannot believe the good news. They flee from the tomb, just as the disciples and the unnamed young man fled from the garden (14.50, 52); and they say nothing to anyone, for they were afraid (*ephobounto gar*). The irony is that until now, men and women who were told to say nothing frequently spoke freely, unable to contain the good news. Now the women are given the best news of all and are told to speak, but apparently say nothing! The human failure which has confronted Jesus throughout Mark's Gospel is there to the very end.

No wonder we find Mark's ending disquieting. We expect him to give us evidence – what we call 'facts' on which to make a judgement. In other words, we expect him to do what the other evangelists do, and tell us how the risen Jesus was seen by his disciples and recognized. We should remember, however, that our expectation of how his Gospel should end is largely shaped by the way in which those other Gospels end: the other evangelists thought it proper to round their stories off with appearances of the risen Jesus, and so we expect Mark to do the same. But Mark was almost certainly the first to write a 'Gospel', and he was creating this particular genre. Though the 'happy ending' seems natural to us, it may not have seemed quite so obvious to Mark that an appearance was necessary. He has already told us that the tomb was empty, and that Jesus had been raised:[14] perhaps he regarded that as the end of the story that was, in effect, only 'the *beginning* of the good news about Jesus Christ' (1.1). From the perspective of a reader who expects a story to be neatly rounded off, however, it seems that Mark has ended at the worst possible place. His abrupt ending would not have been so difficult had he concluded after verse 7, with the young man's announcement of Jesus' resurrection, the reminder of his words, and the command to the women to pass on the message they have been given to the disciples. That would have provided some kind of closure. But he ends with the women's terror, flight and failure to do what they had been commanded. Did he perhaps have some reason for ending just where he did?

Let us look again at the way in which Mark tells his story. His account of what happened begins, in 16.1, with the names of the three women who set out to the tomb early in the morning of the day after the sabbath: they were Mary Magdalene, Mary, the Mother of James, and Salome. The same three women are mentioned in 15.40 as witnesses – together with the centurion – of Jesus' death,[15] while in 15.47, Mary Magdalene and Mary the mother of Joses[16] 'saw where [Jesus' body] was laid'. None of these women has been mentioned previously by Mark, but he explains their presence in 15.41: they had followed Jesus and served him when he was in Galilee, and together with many others, had come up with him to Jerusalem. These women, then, had shown themselves to be true disciples of Jesus by following him and serving him.[17] As witnesses both to the fact that Jesus had indeed died, and to the place of his burial, it was appropriate that they should also be the witnesses to the emptiness of the tomb. But they clearly had no expectation of this as they set out on what appeared to be an absurd mission, to anoint Jesus' body. On the third day after his death, it was already too late for them to do so, and – though they did not know this – it was unnecessary: the only anointing required for his burial had been carried out beforehand (14.8). As though to stress the impossibility of carrying out their intended task, they ask themselves how they are to move the stone (16.3). Their question strikes us as absurd: if they needed help in moving the stone, they should have taken someone stronger with them. The comment that 'it was extremely large' (v. 4) appears to be added as an afterthought. But question and comment alike serve to underline the remarkable fact that the stone had apparently been moved without human intervention.

The women find the tomb empty, and the young man sitting there tells them that Jesus has been raised. Who *is* this young man? Matthew identifies him as an angel, and his white robe might indicate a heavenly origin (cf. Mark 9.3). But Mark refers to him simply as a youth (*neanikos*), the word he used in 14.51 of the man discovered in the Garden of Gethsemane. Another word, clothed (*peribeblē-menos*), gives us a second link with that verse. The first young man had been wearing (*peribeblēmenos*) a linen cloth (*sindōn*), a word often used of a shroud, as it is in 15.46, where it refers to the shroud bought by Joseph of Arimathea for Jesus. Mark's reference to the presence of the young man in Gethsemane is a mystery. Is there some link between him and the young man at the tomb? There is no indication that Mark intends us to identify them, but certainly his language makes us think back to his account of the events that led up to Jesus' death. If that young man was 'suitably dressed' for the events which culminated in Jesus' death, this one is suitably dressed to announce the resurrection.[18]

Even more puzzling than the young man in the Garden, however, is Mark's comment in 16.8 that the women 'said nothing to anyone'. The obvious meaning of the words is that they stayed silent. Once again, there is an interesting echo of an earlier passage, this time of 1.44, where Jesus instructs the leper to 'say nothing to anyone', but to show himself to the priest. Jesus' prohibition here clearly did not exclude speaking to the priest. Could Mark perhaps mean that the women said nothing to anyone *apart from the disciples*? If so, we would expect to be told that they *did* pass on the message to the disciples. It has been suggested that Mark believed that the resurrection had to be proclaimed by the *disciples*, and for this reason the women were not permitted to do so,[19] but this turns what Mark actually wrote on its head, since the women were in fact instructed to 'Go, tell'! All attempts to explain away the women's silence are doomed to failure.

Nevertheless, Jesus' words to the leper in 1.44 are of interest, for here, too, a command is ignored. The instruction to 'say nothing to anyone' contrasts starkly with what we are told then happened, since the leper 'went out and proclaimed it freely and spread the word far and wide'. This is only one of a number of occasions on which Jesus commands silence, and his instruction is ignored.[20] The last such command is given to three disciples after the Transfiguration (9.9). They are instructed to tell no-one what they have seen 'until the Son of man has risen from the dead'. Now that Jesus has been raised, the time to proclaim what has happened has arrived – and the women are silent! Nevertheless, if the 'secret' about Jesus could not be kept secret earlier, we can be certain that God will not allow it to remain hidden now.

For Mark to *end* with the women's silence and fear suggests that these were precisely the things that he wished to stress.[21] It is as though, in challenging his readers to believe, he was knocking away all human props from under them. The disciples do not come to the tomb – only some women, who are the only people (apart from Joseph of Arimathea) who know where Jesus is buried. The women are silent, but who – even had they proclaimed the news to others – would have believed the evidence of *women*? Those who 'see Jesus of Nazareth' will not find him in the tomb, because 'he is not here'. They must look for him *themselves*, and not rely on the evidence of others.

'Jesus is not here' because 'he has been raised'. But where is he? Mark appears to have broken off his story just before what would have seemed the obvious climax, and leaves us waiting to see the risen Lord. But is that not in keeping with what Mark does elsewhere? Throughout his story, he has told us stories that are open to various interpretations. Was Jesus' power given to him by the Holy Spirit or by Satan? (3.20–30). Was he preaching with the authority of God or not? (11.27–33). Was he, or was he not, the Messiah, and Son of God? Mark has hinted at his own interpretation of events, but he has told us repeatedly that men and women refused to believe in Jesus. To grasp the true significance of the story, one has to have eyes and ears of faith. Throughout his narrative, Mark challenges his readers to make the crucial step of faith for themselves. Now, in his closing paragraph, he provides us with some clues: first, an empty tomb; second, a message delivered by the young man to the women; third, a promise that Jesus would appear to the disciples. But the story is open to different explanations, and it is possible to interpret the evidence negatively. How do we know that the message is true? Certainly, Jesus is not in the tomb, but perhaps his body is elsewhere? The message is given by an unknown messenger to women who apparently failed to pass it on, and whose witness was in any case worthless – hardly convincing evidence! But does that mean that the story is false? As for the promise that the disciples will see Jesus, that is apparently unfulfilled. But did it *remain* unfulfilled? Surely not.[22] Even though Mark tells us that the women were too scared to say anything to anyone, it seems that they must eventually have delivered the message to the disciples, for the very fact that the story is now being told shows that it was in fact handed on!

How, then, are we to interpret the evidence? How do we know whether or not the message is true? How do we know whether Jesus has been raised or not? Mark could have told us that Jesus appeared to the disciples, but that would simply tell us how *they* were persuaded that he was alive – it would not necessarily persuade *us*. And Mark's purpose is to persuade *us* of the truth of the gospel – to invite *us* to meet the risen Lord. He therefore gives his readers hints as to how he hopes they will interpret the evidence. The stone, he tells us, had been rolled away – and it was certainly not the women who had done this. The tomb was empty – so where was Jesus to be found? The message entrusted by the young man to the women (v. 7) reminds the disciples that Jesus had promised to precede them to Galilee (14.28); all Jesus' *other* predictions about suffering and death have been fulfilled, so should we not believe this one also? Should we not expect it to be reliable? But the clearest hint of all is in the message sent to the disciples: if they want to see the risen Lord, then they must respond in faith. They must go to Galilee; if they obey, they will see Jesus. Once again, this is just what we might expect after reading the rest of Mark's story. Remember how he commanded a paralytic to get up from his bed (2.11) – an absurd command! How could a paralytic get up? But he has faith, and he obeys. Remember how Jesus told a man with a paralysed hand to stretch it out (3.5) – once again, an absurd command! But this man, too, believes and obeys. Most extraordinary of all, remember how he commanded a dead child to get up from her bed (5.41). Things don't happen *unless* men and women believe and obey: it is because of general unbelief that Jesus healed very few people in his own home town (6.5–6). For Mark, the risen Lord will not be seen unless men and women believe and obey. He might well have concluded with words found in the Fourth Gospel: 'Blessed are those who have not seen and yet have believed.'

But there is one crucial difference between this final paragraph and those earlier episodes in the story: whereas Mark tells us there that the paralysed man got up and walked, that the man with the paralysed hand was able to move it, and the dead child got up from her bed, here he does not tell us that the disciples went to Galilee and met Jesus. So why does Mark break off his story before the obvious climax, and leave us waiting to see the risen Lord? Could it be because he expects us, his readers, to set off ourselves on the journey to see him? Does he perhaps demand that *we* finish the story for ourselves? Mark's ending disturbs us, because it seems so inconclusive. We long to complete the book – and that, of course, is precisely what Mark wants us to do![23] The kind of ending we expect Mark to provide is concrete evidence to persuade us of the truth of Jesus' resurrection. The ending Mark demands that *his readers* supply is the response of faith: it is only those who are prepared to believe and who set off on the journey of faith who will see the risen Lord.[24]

To appreciate what Mark is doing we have to remember that the early Christian communities would not have read this Gospel privately, but would have heard it read aloud. Although we have been referring to his 'readers', we should really speak of his 'hearers'. His Gospel's impact would have been forceful, dramatic, like a play being acted before their eyes. At the very beginning of the story, we met John the Baptist, dressed in camel's hair, standing by the River Jordan, pointing off-stage to someone whom he described as far greater than he was; immediately Jesus appeared on stage. Now, at the very end, we have another young man, dressed in white, pointing off-stage in the direction of Galilee and saying 'Go: tell his disciples that he has gone before you to Galilee; you will see him there.'[25]

But why should they be sent to *Galilee*? Some have suggested that the words of Jesus that are recalled here were not understood by Mark to be a reference to a resurrection appearance at all, but a promise that he would *lead* his disciples into Galilee. 'Galilee' should be understood to symbolize the Gentile world, so that what we have here is a prophecy of the coming Gentile mission spoken of in 13.10.[26] It is true that Isaiah 9.1 refers to 'Galilee of the Gentiles', but while Matthew quotes this passage (Matt. 4.15–16), Mark does not. For Mark, Galilee is the place of Jesus' own ministry, and he gives no hint that he understands it to symbolize something else.

An alternative suggestion is that the saying refers to the Parousia.[27] The promise that the disciples will see (*opsesthe*) the Lord is reminiscent of 'they will see' (*opsontai*) in 13.26 and 'you will see' (*opsesthe*) in 14.62. Both these passages refer to 'the Son of man coming with clouds'. This, moreover, is why Mark stops at verse 8. He cannot describe how the disciples saw Jesus, because the Parousia, when they were to see him, is still awaited.[28] This explanation, too, is unconvincing. Mark 14.28 links the promise with *the resurrection*, and Matthew, an early interpreter of Mark, certainly understood it in that way. Are we to suppose that Mark believed that the disciples were sent to Galilee to await the Parousia, and that they were still there, waiting for Jesus to appear? Since the teaching on the Parousia recorded in Mark 13 emphasizes that 'the end is still to come' (13.7), and explains that before it comes the disciples must proclaim the gospel to the nations (13.10), we have to suppose that the words are addressed to Christians of Mark's own day, and not to the disciples.[29] But why should the Parousia be expected in Galilee? The Mount of Olives would seem to be a far more appropriate venue.[30]

Mark's Ending: Lost or Suspended?

So why Galilee? The most likely explanation is that Jesus' ministry had been based in Galilee. At the beginning of Mark's Gospel (1.14), Jesus came into Galilee, proclaiming the Good News. Now, at the end of the story, the disciples are being told to return. As Mark's first readers heard this message, sent by Jesus via the women, they would have remembered what happened in Galilee when Jesus first called the disciples, and would have realized that this message was a call to begin again on the way of discipleship. But this is an invitation that is addressed to all who hear the story: if they are prepared to follow, they too will see the risen Christ.

The end of Mark's story points us back to the beginning; we have come full circle, and the disciples have to learn the painful lessons of discipleship all over again. This time, in the light of the death and resurrection of the Son of man, they will surely understand his teaching. The words 'just as he told you' force them to think back to what he had taught them. They are to remember what Jesus had said to them, and go back to Galilee. But there are reminders in the young man's message of the story in-between the beginning and the end. Jesus has gone before the disciples (*proagei*), and they need to follow him – just as they did when he went before them (*proagōn*) on the way (*hodos*) to Jerusalem (10.32).[31] On that occasion, those who followed were amazed (*ethambounto*) and afraid (*ephobounto*) because they were not yet fully prepared to tread the way of discipleship. Now the women are amazed (*exethambēthēsan*, v. 5, cf. v. 6), and afraid (*ephobounto*, v. 8). Throughout the Gospel, the disciples had proved slow to learn, and were repeatedly rebuked by Jesus for their hardness of heart;[32] at the crucial moment they failed Jesus completely, since they all forsook him and fled. Peter, to be sure, had summoned up sufficient courage to follow Jesus and his captors at a distance, but had then denied that he was Jesus' disciple. Now, remarkably, they are all given a chance to begin again – and the message is specifically addressed to Jesus' disciples *and Peter*! Peter, who had denied that he was Jesus' disciple is included in the message and told, with them, to remember what Jesus told them: they were, he had said, like sheep, who would be scattered when the shepherd was struck, but when he was raised, then he would go before them into Galilee (14.28). Peter, who had protested that he would never desert Jesus, had been warned of his own coming failure and denial (14.29–31). If we think even further back in the story, we will remember that Jesus had warned would-be disciples that those who were ashamed of him would find that the Son of man would be ashamed of them on the day of judgement (8.38). Remarkably, however, this message at the end of the Gospel assures Peter that Jesus is *not* ashamed to own him as a disciple. He is given another chance. The message to him is, in effect: 'Pick yourself up, Peter. Go back to Galilee, where you were called to be a disciple, and begin again: but now, you will be following the crucified and risen Lord.' The young man's message is not simply the announcement of the resurrection, but the proclamation of the forgiveness that is experienced through Jesus' death and resurrection.

Mark's Gospel ends with human failure. But if Jesus has forgiven the disciples, he will certainly forgive the women for their unbelief. If the power of God has triumphed in spite of human failure and disobedience, it will not be defeated now by their failure to speak. Mark's first 'readers', listening to his words, have themselves heard and responded to the good news of Jesus' resurrection, and know that the women's frailty could not defeat the purpose of God. But they know, too, that neither can their own. For them, too, if they fail, there will be forgiveness. However often the proclamation of the Gospel is met with incomprehension, and however often Christian disciples fail to obey, its message will still triumph. The 'last word' is, after all, the divine proclamation of verse 7, not the human failure of verse 8, since it is always spoken by God.

'Go to Galilee.' The end of Mark's story points us back to its beginning, and reminds us of some of the lessons that we have learned as we have read it. But it points us also into the future, promising all who set out in faith that they, too, will encounter the risen Lord, and assuring them of forgiveness for past failure. The disciples may have failed to follow Jesus to death, and the women may have failed as well, but now others are called to become disciples and to spread the gospel. The young man's message is a command to Mark's readers to follow the same path of discipleship and to pass on the good news to others. Mark's Gospel opened with the words 'The *beginning* of the good news about Jesus Christ'; if the ending to his book is suspended, that is perhaps because the story is still being told in the lives of believers. As he told us in 13.7, 'The end is still to come', and until it does, the story continues. For Mark's readers there is one other promise that is still unfulfilled, and that is the promise of the real end of the story, which arrives only with the Parousia of the Son of man.[33]

Pointing us back to the beginning, Mark's ending is an invitation to reread his Gospel – not *once* more, but again and again. And each time that we read it, we shall discover new insights into his story:

We shall not cease from exploration
And the end of all our exploring
Will be to arrive where we started
And know the place for the first time.

Additional Note: The Later Endings to Mark

It is clear that, even in antiquity, many of Mark's readers were uneasy with his 'suspended' ending. Both Matthew and Luke adapted Mark's account of the visit of the women to the tomb and added further material. Copyists of Mark's Gospel included alternative endings. The shorter of these, found in late Greek manuscripts and in some translations, was very brief indeed. It deals with the problem of the women's silence by flatly contradicting Mark's last sentence, though the outright denial is softened somewhat by the addition of the word 'briefly': 'They reported all these instructions briefly to Peter's companions.' The reference to Peter in verse 7 is here picked up, but Peter is no longer the outsider who needs to be forgiven and included in the group of disciples, but the centre and leader of the community.

One more sentence is added – based, it would seem, on the tradition recorded in Matthew 28.16–20 – telling how Jesus sent out 'the sacred and imperishable proclamation of eternal salvation' to the entire world through 'Peter's companions'. In just a few words, the unknown redactor has brought Mark's story to a conclusion – and to a full stop. The disciples have spread the Good News (now described in Hellenistic terms) throughout the world, and we have our 'happy ending'. Mark's challenge is muted, and there is no longer any pressure on the reader to respond.

Like Mark's own ending, this brief conclusion contains no reference to any appearance of Jesus to the disciples – apart from that which is implicit in the reference to him commissioning the disciples. Perhaps it is not surprising, then, that with one exception,[34] all the manuscripts which include the shorter ending include also the longer. This longer addition is also found *without* the shorter ending in many other manuscripts, though the best of them end at 16.8.[35] The language and syntax of the longer ending are totally un-Markan.[36] Moreover, it is little more than a summary of the appearances described in the other Gospels. Jesus is first seen by Mary Magdalene (vv. 10–11),[37] who passes on the news to the disciples: the difficulty caused by Mark 16.8 is thus explained away. He is then seen by two disciples walking into the country (vv. 12–13),[38] and by the eleven, sitting at table (v. 14).[39] All these brief summaries stress the unbelief of the disciples (vv. 11, 13, 14).

Jesus then commissions the disciples to go out and proclaim the good news (vv. 15–16).[40] To this is added the promise that believers will perform signs which will confirm their message (vv. 17–18, 20), a very different idea from the view expressed in the Gospel itself.[41] The evangelist who refused to give us 'proofs' of the Easter message would surely have been appalled to find someone adding promises of 'signs', intended to confirm the validity of the disciples' words, to his Gospel!

Finally, we are told that the Lord Jesus 'was taken up into heaven and sat down at the right hand of God' (v. 19).[42] The language expresses the later faith of the Church. The disciples then obediently 'went out and preached everywhere, the Lord working with them and confirming their message with signs' (v. 20). As with the shorter ending, the story has been nicely 'rounded off' with the assurance that the disciples have continued Jesus' work, and that the word has been spread. The reader – or listener – can therefore draw a contented sigh and think 'So that's the end of the story.' The challenge of Mark's ending has once again been lost.

3

Matthew's Ending: The Great Commission

To make an end is to make a beginning.

The end is where we start from.

(T.S. Eliot, *Four Quartets*, Little Gidding III)

If Mark's ending is abrupt, that is not entirely surprising for so, too, is his beginning, and indeed his whole story is brief and rushed. Matthew's Gospel is much longer and much tidier: his whole book bears the marks of a teacher, and has clearly been carefully ordered. His introduction is set out with deliberate care. When we turn to the end of the Gospel, we find that he rounds it off in what we may well feel is a more appropriate way; and yet his ending, too, like Mark's, is astonishingly short and *in*conclusive.[1]

Matthew's account of the women's visit to the tomb is clearly based on Mark's, but he makes subtle changes.[2] He names two women only: Mary Magdalene and 'the other Mary' – i.e. the mother of James and Joseph (27.56). Matthew offers no explanation as to *why* they go there, and since he makes no reference to any intention to anoint Jesus' body, he presumably thinks of them as going to the tomb to mourn Jesus' death. In place of the young man in

Mark, who is described simply as dressed in a white robe, and who is merely a messenger, we have an *angel* 'whose appearance was like lightning, and his clothing white as snow' (28.3). This angel plays an active part in what takes place, for while Mark leaves us wondering how the stone had been moved away from the entrance to the tomb, Matthew offers an explanation: there was a great earthquake, and the angel of the Lord descended from heaven and rolled back the stone. Sitting '*on* the stone' (instead of inside the tomb, as in Mark), the angel demonstrates the futility of human attempts to secure the tomb (Matt. 27.62–6). These details stress the divine power which alone could raise Jesus from the dead. It is hardly surprising if Matthew associates supernatural events with the resurrection, since he has already linked the *death* of Jesus with an earthquake and the opening of tombs,[3] and in Matthew's account, it is in reaction to these happenings that the centurion makes his confession: 'Truly, this man was Son of God' (27.50–4).

In Matthew, it is the guards posted at the tomb (about whom Mark says nothing), rather than the women, who are petrified with fear when they see the angel. Matthew describes them as 'like dead men', a phrase which underlines the irony of the situation, since these men were guarding the tomb of someone whom they believed to be dead, but who is now shown to be alive. Presumably he thinks of them as being made unconscious by their experience, and so unaware of the encounter between the angel and the women.[4] Matthew's story had begun with the angel of the Lord urging Joseph not to be afraid to take Mary as his wife; now, at the end, an angel urges the women not to be afraid. They run off – with fear, certainly, but also with great joy – to deliver the angel's message that Jesus has been raised, as he had said, and has gone ahead of the disciples to Galilee (v. 8). On the way, they are met by Jesus himself. Whereas Mark refused to give us any evidence of the resurrection in the form of an appearance, Matthew interrupts his own narrative to describe how the women *saw* the risen Lord, long before he appeared to the disciples. That they should have been the first to see him is remarkable. Mark may well have offended his contemporaries by reporting women to have been the only witnesses of the empty tomb, but Matthew must have scandalized them even more by portraying women as the first witnesses of the risen Jesus.

Yet Matthew agrees with Mark in suggesting that it is those who obey the divine command who will see the Lord: although the women have not yet had a chance to deliver the message, they have obeyed the angel's instruction, for they 'left the tomb quickly to tell the good news to Jesus' disciples' (v. 8). The sight of Jesus confirmed the truth of what they had already believed. They required no further proof: seeing Jesus, they worshipped him. If Jesus – somewhat surprisingly – repeats the angel's message, urging the women once again not to be afraid, and instructing his 'brothers' to go to Galilee, this is presumably *not* because the women are in danger of disobeying the original command, for they have already responded in faith and obedience. They had trusted the angel and obeyed, and their obedience and trust have been rewarded by seeing Jesus. And just as the *sight* of Jesus confirms the angel's message that he has been raised, so now his *words* confirm the second part of that message: the disciples, too, must obey the command to set out in faith. As in Mark, the disciples must go all the way to Galilee if they want to see Jesus; it would seem that *their* faith, unlike that of the women, needs to be tested. Unlike Mark, there is no special mention of Peter, though he is clearly included among those who received the message, since it is 'the eleven' who go to Galilee.

A short account of how the soldiers were bribed by the Jewish authorities to say that the disciples had stolen Jesus' body follows (vv. 11–15). Like his account of how soldiers were appointed to guard the tomb (27.62–6), Matthew's description of how they reported back to the chief priests and Pharisees (28.11–15) serves a dramatic purpose, for just as the setting of the guard filled the gap between Jesus' death and his resurrection, so the soldiers' report allows the women time to pass on the message entrusted to them, and gives the disciples time to set off to Galilee. The story they are bribed to tell is absurd: if they were asleep, how did they know that the disciples had stolen the body? Nor are soldiers likely to have confessed – even when offered a substantial bribe – to sleeping on duty, since that was a capital offence.

But there are more important theological purposes behind Matthew's narrative. Throughout his Gospel, Matthew has emphasized the disbelief of the Jewish authorities, and their responsibility for Jesus' death. Building on Mark's portrayal of the scribes and Pharisees as rejecting Jesus' authority and message, Matthew has added teaching which condemns scribes and Pharisees for their hypocrisy (chapter 23). In the passion narrative, Matthew stressed the guilt of the chief priests and elders by relating the story of Judas's repentance (27.3–10). Judas, he tells us, returned the thirty pieces of silver he had been paid, recognizing that he had betrayed innocent blood, but the chief priests refused to accept them and shrugged off responsibility. Since Judas had thrown down the money in the temple, however, they were forced to do something with it. Because it was 'blood money', it was unlawful to put it in the treasury, and they therefore used it to buy a field, so fulfilling Old Testament prophecy.[5] In Matthew's eyes, the chief priests are unable to deny their responsibility for 'innocent blood'.

In a later passage Pilate, also, claims to be innocent of Jesus' blood (27.24). The chilling response of 'the whole people' was to accept responsibility for his death (v. 25). In this incident, Matthew has portrayed not merely the Jewish leaders but the whole nation as guilty, even though the ultimate responsibility for their rejection of Jesus lies with the chief priests and elders (v. 20). The story of the bribing of the guards in 28.11–15 picks up this theme. This time, the chief priests and elders are responsible for suppressing the truth about the resurrection – even though they had been told 'everything that had happened' by the guards (v. 11). Looking back to 27.62–6, we see the irony of what they do: the guards had been set, at the request of the chief priests and Pharisees, to prevent the disciples stealing Jesus' body and saying that he had been raised. They were anxious, they said, lest the last deception be worse than the first. In the event, it is, but it is *their own* deception, in suppressing the truth about the tomb, that is worse than the first, which was to mislead the crowds and ensure Jesus' death (27.15–23). It is they, therefore, who are once again responsible, not only for their own failure to believe in the resurrection, but also for misleading the Jewish people about what had happened (v. 15).

Matthew's Gospel ends with an extraordinarily brief description of how the disciples went to Galilee, where they met Jesus at the place which he had appointed (28.16–20). This is the first we have heard of Jesus directing the disciples to go to a particular venue, but 'Galilee' is hardly a precise meeting-point, and it is natural if Matthew, in describing the meeting between Jesus and the eleven, should suggest that a precise spot had been indicated. Nevertheless, the term 'the mountain' is clearly symbolic, just as 'Galilee' was for Mark. In 5.1, Jesus had gone up 'the mountain', and it was from there that he had taught the people. It is hardly surprising, then, if Matthew thinks of him as summoning the disciples to the mountain in order to commission them to teach all nations to keep everything that he had taught them (28.20). It was to 'the mountain', moreover, that the Israelites had been summoned to worship God.[6] And it was on a mountain that Jesus had been transfigured in the sight of three of his disciples – an experience about which he had instructed them to keep silent 'until after the Son of man has been raised from the dead' (17.1–9). Did Matthew perhaps think of this command, given as they descended the mountain, as an indication of the place where they would see him after the resurrection?

Standing, now, on the mountain to which they had been summoned, the eleven worshipped Jesus, as the women had done before them, even though – unlike the women – 'they doubted'. Presumably Matthew means that they doubted whether the person whom they now worshipped was indeed Jesus. This is an extraordinary comment on Matthew's part, and it is not made any easier by the fact that it is unclear whether he means that *all* the disciples doubted or only a few of them did.[7] This remark is hardly what we expect if he is trying to offer us proof of the resurrection! Nevertheless, it is typical of what he has told us of the disciples earlier.[8] Particularly interesting is Matthew 14.22–33. This story, like the one in 28.16–20, describes a meeting between Jesus and his disciples, who at first fail to recognize him (v. 26). In the course of their encounter, Peter is rebuked for 'doubting' (14.31), and this is the only other place in the New Testament where the verb, 'to doubt' (*distazō*), used in 28.17, occurs. The basic meaning of the verb is 'to be uncertain', or 'to hesitate', rather than 'to disbelieve', and this is precisely what it means in 14.31. When Jesus first appeared, Peter had already expressed his doubt in the words which he addressed to him, '*if* it is you' (v. 28). Following Jesus' command to come to him, Peter gained sufficient confidence to set out to walk across the water, but then became frightened and began to sink. Jesus rebuked him, not for a total *lack* of faith, but for being 'of *little* faith'. The climax of this incident came when the disciples worshipped Jesus, and acknowledged him to be Son of God (v. 33). Both Matthew 14 and Matthew 28, then, link a hesitant faith with worship.

Since Matthew has deliberately included this reference to the disciples' uncertainty in 28.17, it would seem that he wished to suggest, not that the appearance of the Risen Lord provided incontrovertible proof of the Resurrection, but that those called to follow Christ might well find their faith wavering. Just as Jesus stretched out his hand to Peter, however, so now Christians of Matthew's own day would find that Jesus came to them and reassured *them* (v. 18); whatever their own hesitations, his power was such that they could rely on him.

This resurrection appearance by Jesus to his disciples is the only such scene that Matthew records. In it, Jesus announces that he has been given authority in heaven and on earth, and commissions the disciples to make disciples of all nations, promising to be with them always. They are to pass on everything that he has taught them – an instruction which makes us think back over all the teaching that Matthew has recorded in his Gospel.[9]

And there Matthew leaves us, standing on a mountain with Jesus and the disciples in Galilee; it is, to be sure, a more dignified ending than Mark's; but we are still left wondering what happened next. Are we to think of Jesus disappearing into heaven, as in Luke? What did the disciples do next? We are not told. Once again, the ending forces us to continue the story for ourselves. But this final scene enables Matthew to enlarge upon the themes used by Mark. Unlike Mark, he assures us that the instruction to go to Galilee was obeyed by the disciples, and that they did indeed see Jesus there. In Galilee, they too received a command, given to them – and here is another parallel with the story of the meeting between Jesus and the women – by Jesus himself: they are instructed to go to all the nations, and to make disciples of them all. And just as there is a second command, so there is a second promise. Instead of the promise that they will see Jesus in a particular place (which has now been fulfilled) we have the promise that he will be with them always, even to the end of time,[10] and we may presume that this promise, like the first, will be fulfilled. If Matthew's ending is brief it is because for him, too, the end of the story is only the beginning of what comes next.

But like Mark's ending, Matthew's is appropriate to his story, and picks up ideas which are now familiar to us. In his ministry, Jesus has acted with authority and has claimed that he will exercise authority in heaven[11] as well as on earth;[12] now he claims that authority. In Matthew 9.6, Jesus is said to have claimed authority on earth *as the Son of man*. The authority he is given here seems also to be that of the Son of man (though that title is not used), since the vocabulary echoes the Septuagint of Daniel 7.14.[13] Having endured suffering and death, and been raised from the dead,[14] he now exercises authority.[15] Throughout his ministry, Jesus has been met by both veneration and doubt; now the disciples worship him, in spite of their hesitations. He has called disciples and instructed them into the meaning of discipleship; now he commissions them to make more disciples. The teaching he has given has been what we would expect from a Jewish rabbi, for he has instructed them as to how they should behave;[16] now they are to teach others to observe everything Jesus has commanded them, and it is these practical commands, not doctrine, that they are to pass on, for it is by their obedience to God's will that men and women will be judged.[17] The Jesus whom the disciples meet in Galilee is certainly the same Jesus who has been with them throughout the Gospel.

There is one surprise, however, and that is that the disciples are now commanded to make disciples *of all the nations*. Last time that Jesus commissioned his disciples, he instructed them:

> Do not go on a road that leads to the Gentiles
> Or enter into a city of the Samaritans.
>
> (10.5)

This restriction tallied with the limitation that he is said to have seen to his own mission, as being 'only to the lost sheep of the house of Israel' (15.24). In the past, Jesus has insisted that his mission was to Israel alone. Now a new stage is beginning. It is a stage that will last 'till the end of time' – that is, until the consummation of all things – a phrase that again echoes Jesus' teaching earlier in the Gospel.[18]

There were hints of that future mission earlier. Jesus' mission was said to fulfil the prophecies of Isaiah that promised light, justice and hope for the Gentiles.[19] The disciples, too, were to be 'the light of the world' (5.14); Jesus promised that outsiders would inherit the promises given to Abraham (8.11–12); witness would be made to the Gentiles (10.18; 24.14).[20] But Matthew's ending takes us back, also, to the very beginning of his Gospel, to the first two chapters. There the magi, representatives of the Gentile world, were the first to come and worship Jesus, recognizing him as King even though the Jewish authorities, in the person of Herod, rejected him (2.1–12); we should not be surprised, therefore, if the gospel is now to be taken to the Gentiles. Remarkably, these Gentile magi were said to have been seeking 'the King of the Jews', and to have desired to pay him homage. Although this 'King of the Jews' has now been crucified by Gentiles (27.11, 29, 37), it was once again the *Jewish* leaders, according to Matthew, who rejected him, and who this time succeeded in engineering his death (27.1–2). Now, at the end of the Gospel, *all nations* are to be made disciples (28.19). What was foreshadowed in the opening chapters is about to take place.

The command to baptize seems to introduce a new idea, since nothing has been said until now concerning this. But even this takes us back to the beginning of the Gospel, where we had the account of Jesus' own baptism, when the Holy Spirit descended on him and the Father acknowledged him to be his Son (3.13–17). Now his disciples are to baptize the members of all nations 'in the name of the Father, and of the Son, and of the Holy Spirit' (28.19). If baptism marked the beginning of Jesus' ministry, it will also mark the beginning of something new for these believers.

There are other links between the beginning and the end of Matthew's Gospel. At the very beginning of the story, we were told that the birth of Jesus, who is also named Emmanuel, meaning 'God with us', or 'with us is God', signified the presence of God with his people (1.23).[21] Part-way through, we were told that Jesus used the words that made up the divine name – 'I am' – when he walked on the sea (14.27): the fact that he was exercising divine power in this incident suggests that the allusion is deliberate.[22] Now Jesus echoes the divine name in his final promise: 'I am with you always, to the end of time.' Although this statement forms an *inclusio* with the one in 1.23, the fact that we have come to the end of Matthew's story does not mean that God is no longer with us! Rather, verse 20 marks the beginning of a new era, in which God's presence will be experienced in a new way. In the opening chapters, Matthew described Jesus as God's Son and spoke of the work of the Holy Spirit; now we find Jesus himself referring to the Father, the Son and the Holy Spirit.[23] There, too, we heard how the devil repeatedly tempted him, as Son of God, to exercise his power, and how Jesus insisted that he must obey God. In the final temptation, he was taken to a high mountain and offered all the kingdoms of the world, if only he would worship Satan. Now, on another mountain, we learn that the Son has been *given* the authority he refused to seize, and he is worshipped by the disciples – disciples who had earlier in the story recognized him as 'the Son of the living God' (16.16), but who, like Satan, had tried to tempt him from the path of obedience (16.21–3).

But there is something else – or rather some*one* else – who links the beginning and the end of Matthew, and who influences the middle of the Gospel as well: and that is the figure of Moses. It has frequently been suggested that Moses-typology can be seen in the opening chapters of Matthew; the escape of Jesus from the massacre of the innocents (2.13–18) reminds us of Moses' escape from a similar slaughter by Pharaoh;[24] like Moses, Jesus spends his early years in Egypt. The promise that God would send another prophet like Moses was an important one in Judaism (Deut. 18.15), and it is hardly surprising if Jesus was seen in those terms; but for Matthew, of course, Jesus was much *greater* than Moses. In Matthew's account of the Sermon on the Mount we have a deliberate contrast between Moses, who spoke with God on the mountain and then came down and told the people what God had said, and Jesus, who sat *on* the mountain and taught with far greater authority than even Moses; and in that teaching there is a contrast between the instruction that had been received in the past and what Jesus now told them; a little later in the story we find Jesus on another mountain, the mount of transfiguration, where he talks with Moses and Elijah, and is shown to be superior to them (17.1–8). What happened on that mountain, where Jesus was seen in glory, and the disciples were commanded to obey him, is clearly linked with this final Christophany.

If the superiority of Jesus to Moses is important in the rest of the Gospel, we expect it to be important at the end, for Matthew was attempting to show that Jesus was the true fulfilment of Judaism, as his constant references to the Jewish scriptures, especially in the early chapters, remind us. His story ends with Jesus' final commissioning of his disciples (28.16–20).[25] Some commentators have compared with this passage the stories about the commissioning of Moses' successor, Joshua, in Deuteronomy 31.14–15 and Joshua 1.1–9, suggesting that Matthew's account here is dependent on them.[26] Others have pointed to the 'valedictory' speeches of Moses in Deut. 31.12 and 32.46, in which he commands the people to obey 'all the words of this law'.[27] But the 'words' given by Moses to Israel are not, of course, his own, but the words of God, which he has passed on. Whereas Moses calls on the people to obey the commandments he has been given, Jesus demands obedience to what he himself has commanded the disciples. And though Joshua takes over from Moses, we should note that is not *Moses* who commissions him, but God himself. Now, on the mountain, it is *Jesus* who commissions his disciples, acting with the authority given to him by God, the authority given to him because he is God's Son (28.18–19).

Even more interesting for our purposes is another scene in the Old Testament, with even closer parallels to Matthew 28.16–20, namely the story of the call of Moses in Exodus 3.[28] There we are told how Moses came to Horeb, the mountain of God, where God spoke to him from a burning bush, and commissioned him to bring his people out of Egypt, where they were enslaved. When Moses protested that he was unfit for such a task, God replied, 'but I will be with you', and Moses was then given a sign that God had sent him: he would return to worship God on this same mountain. Since the sign would be nothing less than the successful completion of the task, it was impossible to put God's call to the test without obeying it. But why should Moses trust this God, whom he has never encountered before? He shifts his ground, and asks, 'Who are you, then? What is your name?' And God replies 'I am who I am', a reply which suggests that this God can be known only by those who are prepared to trust him and so discover who he is. But he goes on to remind Moses that he is the God of the patriarchs – of Abraham, Isaac and Jacob (Exod. 3.15; cf. 3.6). Moses is called on to trust the God who has commissioned him, but he does know that he has revealed himself to his forefathers.[29]

For Matthew, Jesus is far greater than Moses; their infancy stories may have seemed alike, but now the two figures have parted, and in this last scene we see that there is a significant difference between them. For clearly Jesus is not the one who is commissioned, but *the one who commissions others;*[30] it is therefore *Jesus* who summons the disciples to the mountain which he had appointed, just as God summoned the Israelites to go to the mountain which *he* had appointed. The disciples' journey to meet Jesus, who was now – incredible as it might seem – rumoured to be alive, was as great an act of faith as was the journey of the Israelites to Horeb. The Israelites were summoned to the mountain to worship God there, and their arrival was to be the only proof that Moses would be given that God had sent him. Now the disciples worship Jesus on the mountain, even though some doubt, just as Moses had doubted God's call and the Israelites had doubted God's power. When Moses brought the people to the mountain God spoke to him again, and Moses then taught the people to observe everything that God commanded him (Exod. 19.3–8). Now Jesus tells the disciples that *they* are to teach men and women to observe everything that *he* has commanded them. Their mission is no longer confined to Israel, however, but includes the Gentiles; we are reminded of the rabbinic legend which tells us that God summoned all the nations to receive the Law on Mount Sinai, but that the Jews alone responded;[31] now all the nations are to receive the words of Jesus.[32] Moses had demanded to know God's name, and he was told that 'I am' had sent him (Exod. 3.14); the name of God which is now revealed to the disciples is that of Father, Son and Holy Spirit.

The story in Exodus ends with a reminder of God's commission of Moses, who is sent to Pharaoh with the words 'I am has sent you' ringing in his ears; now Jesus sends his disciples out with the promise: 'I am with you always, to the end of time.' Jesus is no longer seen simply as greater than Moses, but as one who acts with the authority of God and as the bearer of the divine Name. No wonder the Jewish authorities denounced the Christian claims as blasphemous! But if we want to see the story from Matthew's point of view, then we have to understand that for him it is the God who commissioned Moses who now speaks through the risen Jesus.

Earlier in the Gospel, Jesus made another promise to his disciples: 'where two or three are gathered in my name, I am there among them' (18.20). His words are illumined by a saying in the rabbinic writings: 'If two sit together and words of the Law [are spoken] between them, the Divine Presence rests between them.'[33] This promise to be with his followers reminds us again of the fact that he is Emmanuel, 'God with us', the name given to him at his conception (1.23). Now, at the end of the Gospel, this truth is reaffirmed, for he assures his disciples: 'I am with you till the end of time.' This final scene in Matthew is not just a commissioning: it is a Christophany – a revelation of who Jesus is – and his final promise to those whom he sends out echoes the promise of Yahweh to Moses.

It seems unlikely that these echoes of Moses are accidental. If they are deliberate, they remind us that the beginning of Matthew's story is not to be found in Bethlehem of Judaea, nor even in the call of Moses, but in the revelation of the God who calls himself 'I am' to Abraham, Isaac and Jacob (Exod. 3.15). It is hardly surprising, then, that he begins his Gospel with a genealogy which traces the lineage of Jesus back to Abraham. And the end of the story will be told only when Jesus' followers have evangelized the whole world, for his significance is universal: the small group of eleven is to be expanded to include all nations! Although Matthew has continued his narrative further than did Mark, and has given us witnesses to resurrection appearances (to a couple of women, and to eleven disciples), he has given us very little more in the way of solid evidence! Even the disciples were hesitant – though the women were not.

Like Mark's, Matthew's ending, also, is a 'suspended' one: 'it invites the reader to enter the story'.[34] Jesus promises that from now on, he will be with his people. But what *sounds* like a benediction – 'I am with you always, to the end of time' – proves to be his marching-orders to the disciples to take the gospel to the nations. It is only by obeying those orders that they will discover that Jesus is, indeed, the risen Lord who is with them. For Matthew, the end of his 'Gospel' was also the beginning of its proclamation to the world: the 'good news' had to be shared. Like Mark, Matthew appears to have ignored Aristotle's dictum that 'an end . . . has nothing following it'.[35] For them both, it would seem that, in Eliot's words,

To make an end is to make a beginning.
The end is where we start from.

4

Luke's Loose Ends

There is no end, but addition.

(T.S. Eliot, *Four Quartets*, The Dry Salvages II)

Mark's Gospel gives the impression of having been written by a man in a hurry; its author rushes from one scene to another until, at the end, he takes his leave abruptly, leaving his hearers to make the next move. His style of writing is matched by his knowledge of Greek, which is basic and unrefined – colloquial rather than literary. The abrupt ending to his Gospel is thus of a piece with the rest of the book. Yet it leaves us uneasy. Is it, as some maintain, simply the result of a clumsy writer's incompetent work, or is it, as I suggested, a profound theological challenge – a compelling invitation to carry on the story? Matthew's story is more measured, with the material carefully arranged in blocks. His ending, though more polished than Mark's, nevertheless leaves his readers wondering what happened next.

When we turn to Luke's Gospel, we find a very different document: almost twice as long as Mark's, this book is written in excellent Greek by someone who was a master of the language. Luke tells his story slowly, carefully and elegantly. When we reach the end of the Gospel, therefore, we expect something far more smooth and cultured. And since

48

his Gospel comes to a clear end, there is a sense in which we are not disappointed. Yet he, too, puzzles us by leaving loose ends, which he fails to tie up. Why? Is he simply careless, or has he *deliberately* left pieces of his narrative incomplete?

In Luke, as one scholar has put it, Jesus stands in 'the Middle of Time'.[1] The whole of Luke's Gospel looks back to what God has done in the past and forward to what God is going to do in the future, and nowhere is this clearer than in the introduction and conclusion. Mark begins his story by quoting scripture, declaring that the words written in Isaiah are now being fulfilled. Luke makes this point even more clearly, for his first two chapters borrow the language and phraseology of the Jewish scriptures, as though to remind us that the story he is telling us is the continuation of a story begun long before[2] – so long before that when Luke traces the genealogy of Jesus, he goes back not simply to Abraham, as does Matthew, but to Adam. The very first story in the book – the account of how John the Baptist was conceived and born – echoes the story of Hannah and Elkanah and the birth of Samuel in 1 Samuel 1 and 2. The God who has been at work in the history of his people Israel is still at work.

But what is God doing? The announcements made by angels, who appear to Zechariah, to Mary and to the shepherds, together with the hymns and songs found in the mouths of inspired prophets – Zechariah, Mary and Simeon – explain the significance of what is taking place, and tell us also what God is going to do, through the child born to Mary. The coming of Jesus brings salvation to his people Israel,[3] and there is a promise, also, of salvation for the

Gentiles.[4] And when we turn to the *concluding* chapter, we find that this, like the last chapter in Mark, looks back to what has happened and forward to what is going to happen. The beginning and ending are like book ends, holding the whole narrative together, but these book ends do not simply enclose the narrative, for they also point backwards and forwards, to the story that began long ago and that still continues. Jesus stands 'in the Middle of Time'.

That Luke's story continues after the end of chapter 24 is obvious for another reason, since there is one notable difference between what we have in Mark and Matthew on the one hand, and what we have in Luke on the other: Luke has a second volume. In spite of the fact that he gives us a more satisfying ending than does Mark, the end of his Gospel is very clearly *not* the end of the story, for this first volume is, to use the opening words of volume two, 'an account of what Jesus *began* to do and to teach'. The story continues until at least the end of Acts, for in this second volume we find that the apostles follow in Jesus' footsteps. In his Gospel Luke makes plain, by his use of the Old Testament, that the story of Jesus is the continuation of what has happened in the past, and in Acts he makes plain that the story of the apostles is the continuation of the story of Jesus. Like him, they proclaim the kingdom of God,[5] they perform similar miracles,[6] and some of them suffer persecution and even death.[7] Not surprisingly, then, as though to alert us to this idea, the end of the Gospel looks forward to things that happen in Acts, and Acts looks back at what has happened in the Gospel; even more interestingly, the end of volume one and the beginning of volume two overlap. Writing two volumes, it is hardly surprising if the second picks up themes from the first, so that taken together they fulfil Eliot's expectation that ' . . . the beginning shall remind us of the end'.[8] Acts opens with a brief recapitulation of the Gospel of the kind customary in contemporary two-part literary works,[9] reminding us that Luke has already written an account of 'all that Jesus did and taught, from the beginning until the day when he was taken up to heaven'. Moreover, this recapitulation is followed by a retelling of the final events in the Gospel, rather in the way that happens today, if we are watching or listening to a two-part television or radio drama; at the beginning of part two, we expect to be given a résumé of the previous instalment, followed by the closing scene. Disconcertingly, however, when the closing scene of the Gospel is recalled in Acts, it appears to have been 'refilmed' in the time since Luke wrote the original account, for the two versions of the ascension are somewhat different.

Luke has often been described as an historian, and one of the issues that New Testament scholars continue to debate is whether or not this is an appropriate description of a writer whose concern is to relate what God has done in and through Jesus and his disciples. His books certainly have many similarities with some of the historical books in the Jewish scriptures – though it should always be remembered that they, too, were records of what God had done in the history of his people.[10] Among these, we may observe an interesting parallel between the way in which Luke and Acts overlap and similar overlaps which occur between the first and second books of Kings, and between 2 Chronicles and Ezra–Nehemiah; in both these cases, the last story in one book is repeated in the next, as though to make sure

that readers understand that the second volume is a continuation of the story told in the first. Was Luke deliberately following that model? If he was, that would not be
surprising, for as we have already noted, the opening
chapters of the Gospel are soaked in Old Testament language, and he certainly uses the Jewish scriptures as his
model in other ways.[11]

It would seem, then, that Luke did his best to ensure that
his readers recognized that his two volumes belonged
together. Sadly, however, generations of readers missed the
point! Because Luke's Gospel and Acts were separated
from each other when our New Testament was put
together, the link between them has frequently been over-
looked. For Luke, however, his two books were rather like
one of those continental trams, made up of two carriages,
separate and yet firmly linked together, with both carriages
heading inextricably for the same destination. It is not surprising, then, that the ending of Luke, like the ending of
Mark, points forward to the next stage of the story, and
that the beginning of Acts makes that plain; and when we
turn to the end of Acts, we shall need to ask whether we
find the same phenomenon occurring there also, and
whether that points forward to what happens next.

But let us begin with the Gospel. Luke was a literary
man; of all the evangelists, it was he who wrote the most
elegant Greek and who knew how to tell a story. The ending of his Gospel is a far more polished piece than that of
Mark, and he may well have been relying on another source
in preference to Mark. He tells the story of the women's
visit to the tomb with subtle variations (24.1–11); the
women bring spices, find that the stone has been rolled

away from the tomb, and are confronted by two men in dazzling clothes, who rebuke them for seeking the living among the dead. Instead of being given a message to deliver, they are addressed directly, and the disciples are not directed to return to Galilee, as in Mark. Instead, the women are themselves reminded of the words Jesus had spoken to them *in* Galilee about his own death and resurrection (24.6). The words of the men dressed in dazzling clothes, whom they meet at the tomb – in Luke there are two, not one, as in Mark – serve to jog *our* memories also, for they remind us of the earlier chapters of the book. Luke tells us that the women 'remembered Jesus' words' (24.8): does he mean that because they remembered what Jesus had said, they therefore believed the words of the angels? When they realized that Jesus' words about his death had been fulfilled, did they conclude that what he had said about rising again must also be true? If so, then they apparently believed *without* seeing Jesus. Certainly they return to the eleven and tell them all that they have seen and heard, and it is the disciples, not the women, who fail, since they cannot believe what they are told, and regard what the women say as 'an idle tale' (24.11). Peter rushes to the tomb to see for himself, sees exactly what the women have reported, and is amazed (24.12).[12]

The major difference from Mark, however, is the fact that Luke reports sightings of Jesus, both of which are centred on Jerusalem. First, we have the story of the walk to Emmaus (24.13–35): two disciples encounter the risen Jesus, but do not recognize him, so they tell him about what has happened; their hopes that Jesus was the promised redeemer of Israel have been dashed with his crucifixion, but wild rumours are circulating that the tomb has been found empty and that angels have told some women that he is alive (24.19–23). We who read the story appreciate the irony of these words, for we know that they are unwittingly telling Jesus his own story, and that Luke is writing about these events precisely because he believes them to prove that Jesus is indeed the promised redeemer of Israel, whose coming was heralded by Zechariah and Anna (1.68; 2.38).

Then, beginning with Moses and the prophets, Jesus explains to the two disciples how the whole of scripture pointed forward to himself (24.25–7). The travellers' account of recent events and of their own hopes force us to think back over the whole story of Jesus as Luke has told it, while the words of Jesus make us see that story in a new light. Now, as he breaks bread, reminding them – and us – of similar occasions, the two disciples recognize him, and he vanishes from their sight (24.30–1).[13] Their failure until this point to recognize Jesus is striking: it is only when faith dawns that their eyes are opened and they finally *see* him – and then he disappears. What is *really* important is that they should grasp that 'it was *necessary* for the Messiah to suffer these things and to enter into his glory' (v. 26), and to recognize his presence with them in the breaking of bread (vv. 30–1) and the unfolding of scripture (v. 32). The fact that they recognize Jesus in Emmaus, several miles from Jerusalem, is a pattern for future believers: they do not need to visit the tomb, or to be in Jerusalem, in order to be in the presence of the risen Lord. This story, like the first one, has a postscript about Peter, though he is referred to as 'Simon', presumably because he has failed to live up to his name: the two travellers rush back to Jerusalem, and are greeted by the disciples with the words 'The Lord has indeed risen, and has appeared to Simon' (24.34).

In Jerusalem, Jesus now appears to the disciples, who react with fear (vv. 36–7), as had the women (v. 5), but also with disbelief and amazement (v. 41), just as they had done when they received the women's report (vv. 11 and 12). Seeing Jesus and believing in him are clearly not necessarily synonymous. The disciples take him to be a ghost, so he invites them to touch him, and then eats fish to convince them that he has 'flesh and bones' (vv. 37–43). Jesus reminds them once again of what he has taught them – that is, that what was written about him in scripture in the law of Moses, the prophets and the psalms – had to be fulfilled (vv. 44–7). Once again we are being reminded of what has already been said, but this time the twin ideas in the previous two stories are brought together, for we are being pointed back *both* to the teaching of Jesus about which Luke has been telling us (cf. vv. 6–7), *and* to the scriptures (cf. v. 27), written long before Luke's story began.[14]

All these stories, then, emphasize that what has happened was the divine plan: it was necessary for everything written in the scriptures about the Messiah to be fulfilled, and Jesus had been fully aware of this. In this final story, the scriptures are said to refer, not simply to Jesus' death and resurrection, but to the repentance and forgiveness of sins which will be proclaimed in his name: what John the Baptist had preached to Israel (3.3) is now proclaimed to all the nations (24.47). Then Jesus commissions the disciples to be his witnesses and to proclaim the gospel,[15] and says that he will send them the promise of his Father – that is, the Holy Spirit (24.48–9) – yet another reminder of what John the Baptist had announced at the beginning of the Gospel (3.16). He leads them out to Bethany, blesses them and once again vanishes from sight (24.50–1).[16]

The last sentence in the Gospel is reminiscent of the fairy-tale ending, for all ends happily. Since the Messiah had now 'entered into his glory', the disciples 'returned to Jerusalem with great joy, and spent all their time in the temple praising God' (24.52–3). Luke has brought us back, full circle, to where he began his story, in the temple in Jerusalem: the great joy experienced by the disciples echoes the words of the angels to Zechariah and to the shepherds,[17] and like Zechariah and like Simeon, the disciples praise God;[18] their constant worship in the temple reminds us of Anna, who worshipped there night and day.[19] The expectations aroused at the beginning of the Gospel seem to have been fulfilled. And Jesus himself is now plainly revealed to be the Messiah (26.46) and the Lord (v. 34), as announced in chapters 1 and 2.[20]

In fact, however, this is no cosy fairy-tale ending, for the disciples are not going to be allowed to settle down to domestic bliss. There is certain unfinished business which Luke spelt out at the beginning of the Gospel, but which has mysteriously remained unfulfilled. At the beginning of the story, there was a promise of salvation for the Gentiles;[21] what has happened to that? One of the strange features of Luke's Gospel is that there is little in it to suggest that Jesus helped Gentiles.[22] Why? Has Luke forgotten what was promised in the opening chapters? And what has happened to the promise found a little later in the story – the promise that Jesus will baptize with the Holy Spirit?[23]

Jesus now commissions the disciples to take the gospel to the world – that is, to the Gentiles – and renews the promise about the Holy Spirit, but the book closes before either of these events takes place. Here, then, are two expectations still awaiting fulfilment – two loose ends, waiting to be fulfilled.[24]

Scholars have often asked, 'Did Luke intend to write a second volume when he wrote the first?' The fact that he did nothing in volume one to show how Jesus' coming brings salvation to the Gentiles suggests that he did, for he knew that the preaching of the gospel to the Gentiles belonged to the next stage in the story. But there is a third important loose end which also demands to be tied up. Back in the early chapters of the Gospel, the insistent theme of those inspired people who spelt out the meaning of what was happening with the coming of Jesus was that it meant salvation for Israel; the emphasis was on the fulfilment of God's promises to his people, and the salvation of the Gentiles was, as it were, a spin-off from that event. Now we have come to the end of the Gospel, and it closes with a commission to go to the Gentiles. The promise about them is about to be fulfilled – provided that the disciples obey their marching orders. The promise about the Holy Spirit has been repeated. But where is the promised salvation for Israel? The two disciples *en route* to Emmaus echoed that promise when they spoke of their hope, now apparently shattered, that Jesus was the one who would redeem Israel (24.21). So what has happened to that redemption? Luke's ending, apparently so much tidier than Mark's, has left us, as did his, waiting expectantly for what will happen next.

And when we turn to the very first scene of Acts, we find that Luke's three loose ends are all picked up.[25] The book begins – as the Gospel ended – in and near Jerusalem. Jesus' final instructions to his disciples in 1.3–8 repeat those in Luke 24: he first promises them that they will very shortly receive the gift of the Holy Spirit – a promise which is almost immediately fulfilled (Acts 2.1–4). He goes on to elaborate his commission to them to be his witnesses – in Jerusalem, in all Judaea and Samaria, and to the ends of the earth.[26] The rest of the book tells the story of how the apostles took the gospel not only to Jews but to Gentiles, beginning in Jerusalem, then in Judaea and Samaria, and finally much further afield.

That leaves us with our third loose end, the promise in Luke 1–2 to redeem Israel, the promise picked up by the disciples on the way to Emmaus, who had hoped that Jesus was the one who would redeem Israel. We have some sympathy with the disciples when they interrupt Jesus to ask, 'Is this the time when you will restore the kingdom to Israel?' But their hope is thrown yet further into the future when he replies that they cannot know the time when this will take place (Acts 1.6–7). As we read on through Acts we find that Jesus' final words about the Holy Spirit and the mission to the nations are being fulfilled: indeed, the whole book tells of how the Gentiles respond to the gospel and receive the Holy Spirit. But Jews are repeatedly shown as rejecting the gospel. What, then, has happened to the apparently unfulfilled promises about the salvation of Israel, set out in the early chapters of Luke?[27]

For an answer, let us turn to the final page of Acts, and see how Luke ends his second volume: has he perhaps now,

at last, brought his story to a conclusion, and finally tied up
all the loose ends? Paul, we discover, has come to Rome as
a prisoner, though he is allowed to live in his own lodgings
(28.16). What took place there provides not only interesting echoes of the account of the trial of Jesus at the end of
the Gospel,[28] but interesting echoes, also, of the beginning
of Acts. Paul's account of how he comes to be in Rome in
28.17–20 summarizes what has happened in chapters
22–6.[29] As we take leave of Paul, he is proclaiming the kingdom of God and teaching about Jesus (28.31) – a neat
example of *inclusio*, since in Acts 1.3, Jesus himself spent
forty days instructing the disciples about the kingdom of
God. But of course this link takes us back to the Gospel as
well, for as Acts 1.1 reminds us, it was in his *first* volume
that Luke told us of all that Jesus himself began to do and
to teach. As with Mark, we are being forced to go back and
reread the Gospel.

And yet the ending of Acts is something of a disappoint-
ment. The book itself has told a story of epic proportions
and high drama: lynchings, riots, narrow escapes, ship-
wrecks, assassination plots; and now at last Paul has made
his way to Rome, the capital of the Empire. We expect a
grand climax. And how does Luke end? 'Paul lived there
two whole years at his own expense . . . proclaiming the
kingdom of God and teaching about Jesus Christ openly
and without hindrance.' Once again we turn the page,
expecting to find more, and once again, we discover only
a blank. This ending is almost as abrupt as Mark's. What
kind of conclusion is this? Have Luke's literary skills
deserted him?

Many explanations have been offered as to why Luke

should end at this point.[30] Perhaps, it is suggested, he intended to write a third volume. Well, perhaps, but it would surely have been little more than a brief postscript to the other two. And would we not expect Luke to round off volume two a little more neatly? Perhaps he had brought the story up to date, and there was no more to tell, since Paul was still in detention in Rome. Well, perhaps, but that causes problems with the dating not only of Acts but of all the Gospels as well, since Luke was clearly written before Acts, and Luke is almost certainly dependent on Mark: although it is impossible to date Acts with any confidence, it must certainly have been written well after AD 70.[31] Perhaps Luke shirked from telling the tale of Paul's martyrdom. That seems unlikely, since he had not shirked from telling us of Jesus' death. And after all, it is clear how Paul's story is going to end; there have been sufficient indications of what was inevitable to leave us in no doubt of the outcome of his trial.[32] Perhaps, it is suggested, Luke did not wish to describe Paul's execution because that would conflict with his attempts elsewhere to show Roman rule as just and impartial. But breaking off the story at this point is no answer to this problem, since everyone would have known the outcome (or would have demanded to know what it was if they did not!). There is, to be sure, a tradition that Paul was released and continued his missionary work, but Luke shows no knowledge of that, and the predictions of his fate[33] seem to demand that Paul's imprisonment ended in his death.

Why, then, did Luke break off the story with Paul a prisoner in Rome? Could there be some *positive* explanation? It has been pointed out by others[34] that there is an intriguing parallel between the end of 2 Kings and the end of Acts. At the end of 2 Kings the last of the kings of Judah, Jehoiachin, is released from prison in Babylon, but remains in that city, confined to court, a symbol of the unfulfilled hope of Israel for the restoration of the kingdom. Paul is no king, but he *is* a prisoner in Rome on account of the hope of Israel (28.20).[35] Has Luke seen a parallel?

And has Luke perhaps drawn a deliberate parallel between the end of his Gospel, where the disciples return to Jerusalem, the centre of Israel's worship, and spend their time in the temple, praising God and waiting to begin their missionary work, and the end of Acts, where Paul is in Rome, the centre of the Gentile world, in his own lodgings, proclaiming the kingdom of God and teaching about Christ to everyone who comes to him? The content of his teaching picks up themes from Luke 24, where Luke tells us that the risen Jesus rebuked his disciples for not grasping what the scriptures said about himself (Luke 24.25), and that he interpreted Moses, the prophets and the psalms to them (24.27, 32, 44–7). Now Paul, in turn, expounds the scriptures to the Jews (Acts 28.23), trying to convince them about Jesus, and rebukes them for *their* unbelief (28.25–8). At the end of the Gospel, the disciples are in Jerusalem, praising and waiting; at the end of Acts, the good news about Jesus has reached Rome, and is being proclaimed to all comers. The story has certainly advanced! But it is not yet concluded, because not all believe, and not all have yet heard.

The loose ends have not yet been tied up, because the end has still not come: but in the meantime, the Holy Spirit is at work – for what the Spirit said through Isaiah is being effected (v. 25), the Gentiles are responding to the gospel (v. 28) and Paul himself suffers imprisonment for the hope of Israel (v. 20).

Luke's ending has seemed to many to be a damp squib, as feeble as the end of Mark's Gospel; but others have described it as a 'triumphant and effective conclusion'.[36] We have already seen that Mark's ending may not be as feeble as it appears, so is it possible that the end of Acts is similarly effective? Let us have another look at Luke's closing scene.[37] Paul arrives in Rome, which has been for so long his goal,[38] summons the Jews to his house and explains his situation: 'it is', he tells them, 'on behalf of the hope of Israel that I am in these chains' (v. 20).[39] Then he speaks to them about the kingdom of God and tries to convince them about Jesus from the Law of Moses and the prophets. Some are convinced and others refuse to believe, whereupon Paul quotes the much-used words of Isaiah 6: 'You will listen, but never understand; you will look but never see,'[40] and declares that God's salvation had been sent to the Gentiles.

In this scene, Luke reminds us that Paul is proclaiming the kingdom of God – the kingdom which Jesus himself was sent to proclaim (Luke 4.43), and for which the disciples are shown to be waiting at the end of the Gospel and the beginning of Acts, expecting it to manifest itself through the restoration of Israel.[41] He shows us Paul explaining about Jesus from Moses and the prophets, just as the risen Jesus had done in Luke 24.27 and 44. Paul, therefore, is continuing both the teaching of Jesus and the mission entrusted to the disciples in the opening scene of Acts – the mission to proclaim the gospel. But equally important, we are reminded that the gospel is about *the hope of Israel*. What *is* this hope? Several times in the course of Acts Paul has referred to the hope he shares with his fellow-Jews (or some of them, since the hope was not shared by Sadducees) – that is, hope in the resurrection.[42] Moreover, it is specifically for this hope that he is on trial.[43] He is not, of course, on trial simply for holding this hope (though 23.6–10 might suggest this to be the case), but rather for claiming that it has been fulfilled in the person of Christ. It seems likely that the reference to the hope of Israel in 28.20 is also to the resurrection hope, but it is probable that here, as elsewhere, it is primarily a way of making contact with fellow-Jews, and establishing that the gospel is the fulfilment of Jewish hopes, not a denial of them. The next step would be to explain that this hope of resurrection had been confirmed in the resurrection of Christ. The light which brings revelation to the Gentiles is the realization of the promises made to Israel, and so destined to be the glory of Israel, just as we were told in Luke 2.32. Even what seems like uncompromising failure, in the fulfilment of Isaiah 6, has to be seen in the light of this reference to the hope of Israel.

Now the strange thing about this encounter between Paul and the Jews in Rome is that it is the third time this particular scene has occurred in Acts.[44] Three times Luke has told us that Paul preached the gospel to the Jews, and finding his message rejected, turned to the Gentiles.[45] We are used to thinking of Paul as the apostle to the Gentiles, which is how he describes himself in his letters, but Luke thinks of him as called to preach to both Jews and Gentiles.[46] And he goes on doing so until the very end. The

notion that the Jews have been rejected is foreign to Acts:
however often Paul throws up his hands in despair and says
he will try a more promising opening, we find him attempting to persuade the Jews of the truth of his gospel.[47]
Moreover he persuades some of them! 'Some were convinced,' says Luke in v. 24, 'while others resisted.'[48] As
though to emphasize this mixed response, someone at some
stage added v. 29, which describes how the Jews continued
to argue vigorously among themselves.[49]

Is Acts a triumph or a damp squib? Certainly not a damp
squib! What we have is a reaffirmation of the triumph to
come. The march of the gospel continues, and has reached
as far as Rome. Some Jews do accept the gospel, and
though others reject it, that serves only to confirm Paul in
his conviction that the gospel is meant also for the
Gentiles.[50] His final words to the Jews are an affirmation of
this fact:

> Let it be known to you, therefore, that this salvation of
> God has been sent to the Gentiles; and they will listen.

Moreover, this picks up themes from Luke's prologue to his
Gospel, which was written, he told Theophilus, so that *he*
might '*know* the truth concerning the things' about which
he had been informed (1.4); this Gospel, moreover, was
concerned with *God's salvation*, which would bring the
light of revelation to the Gentiles (2.30–2). What had been
promised at the beginning of Luke's first book is now
taking place: at one and the same time, we are being
reminded of the beginning of the story, and being pointed
once again towards the future. Luke's own final words tell

us that Paul continued in Rome for two whole years, preaching the gospel openly and without hindrance! The real reason why Luke ends here is surely that he has reached what is for him the climax of the story – and that climax is *not* the death of Paul. What happens to the gospel is for Luke far more important than what happens to Paul.[51] He wishes to end his narrative, not with Paul's execution, but with the unfettered proclamation of the gospel.[52]

Like our other conclusions, this is clearly a suspended ending. We are not told about Paul's fate; we are left wondering about the promised programme of Acts 1: the gospel has not yet been taken to *all* the nations,[53] the hope of Israel has not been fully realized, nor has Jesus returned to earth in the same way that he left. For Luke, the story of salvation is still being told, and since that story began in the Old Testament, it is a story *that concerns the salvation of God's people Israel.* How *can* Luke conclude this story *except* with a suspended ending? He leaves his readers to write the next pages for themselves. Just as the book of Genesis ends with Joseph on his death-bed in Egypt, assuring Israel that God will bring his people into the land he promised to Abraham, Isaac and Jacob, and just as the book of Deuteronomy ends with Moses on Pisgah, looking out over the Promised Land, so Acts ends with Paul confident that the gospel will be taken to the ends of the earth.[54]

If some commentators do not appreciate this kind of ending, is it perhaps because they have been too much influenced by the great romantic novels, where everything is neatly sorted out?[55] Chrysostom, writing on Acts, was more appreciative of what the author was trying to do, and hints that in the ancient world the ending might not have seemed unusual.[56] He writes:

> At this point the historian stops his account and leaves the reader thirsting, so that thereafter he guesses for himself. This also non-Christian writers do. For to know everything makes one sluggish and dull.[57]

Scholars differ, as we have noted, in their opinions as to whether or not Luke is properly described as an historian, and whether, if he is, he was a *good* historian. Whatever the truth on this matter, he was surely something much more important: he was a good preacher. If he stops his account and leaves us, his readers, as Chrysostom expresses it, 'thirsting' for more, it is not because he wants us to guess about what happened next, but because he wants us to continue the story for ourselves. In effect, he is saying: at this point, it's a matter of 'Over to you'. The Holy Spirit has been poured out, and the nations are responding, but the time for the restoration of God's kingdom has not yet arrived, and until it does, *you* must be Christ's witnesses, in Jerusalem, in Judaea and Samaria, and to the ends of the earth. For Luke, then,

There is no end, but addition.

5

John: Endings and Beginnings

In my beginning is my end

. . .

In my end is my beginning.

(T.S. Eliot, *Four Quartets*, East Coker I, V)[1]

The Fourth Gospel, like the Gospel of Matthew, reflects a situation in which the Christian community is in conflict with the Jewish synagogue. Its author, like Matthew, claims that Jesus is the true embodiment of the revelation that God has given to his people in the past in the Torah – the teaching entrusted to Moses – and to support this, John endeavours to demonstrate, in the series of 'signs' and 'discourses' related in John 2–12, that God is more fully known in Jesus than in the worship of the temple and the synagogue. John's Gospel is very different from the Synoptics, containing very different material, and being written in a distinctive style, and yet it is also similar, for it is recognizably a Gospel, as are they, and it tells the story of Jesus' ministry, concluding with his death and resurrection. Like the other Gospels, this one has an introduction – or 'prologue' – which provides a key to understanding the significance of the story (John 1.1–18). And like the other

Gospels, it ends with stories about the empty tomb and (*unlike* Mark) with accounts of appearances.

It would not have been entirely surprising if John had *not* thought it necessary to conclude in this way – if, like Mark, he had ended his Gospel with the story of the empty tomb, or even with the death of Jesus. For after all, John has spoken of the crucifixion of Jesus as his exaltation[2] and his glorification,[3] and has portrayed him as dying with the triumphant words 'It is finished' on his lips (John 19.30). After this, do we really *need* stories of appearances? The evangelist's own account of what took place following the resurrection will point out that belief should *not* be dependent on seeing the risen Lord. Surprisingly, however, John includes more accounts of resurrection appearances than any of the other evangelists. These final chapters serve to remind us of the various passages which have spoken of Jesus' coming resurrection and its significance, and describe incidents that confirm their truth. The promises made by Jesus to his disciples that they would see him again, and that if he left them he would return, have been fulfilled.[4] Now, at last, they come to understand the meaning of his puzzling words about a temple that will be rebuilt (John 2.19–22).

The Gospel's ending is, as we might expect, at once familiar and yet strange. In John 20 an unfamiliar version of the story of the empty tomb records how Mary Magdalene visited it – on her own – and found that the stone had been removed. Presumably she looked inside and found it empty, since she reported to Peter and 'the disciple whom Jesus loved' that Jesus' body had been removed from the tomb. Peter and the beloved disciple then rushed to the tomb to see for themselves; Peter blundered in and examined the evidence, but when the other disciple went in, he 'saw and believed'. In this story, the fourth evangelist spells out what Mark's abrupt conclusion implies: appearances are not necessary for belief. Faith should not depend on *seeing the risen Lord*: although the beloved disciple saw the empty tomb he did not need to see or hear Jesus himself – or even an angel – in order to believe. He is thus a model for all those future disciples who believe in the risen Lord without actually seeing him – those who are said, in verse 29, to be blessed because they have come to believe in Christ *without* seeing him.[5]

This story is followed by three appearances of the risen Jesus, all of them set in Jerusalem. The first of these is to Mary; once again, we find an evangelist boldly maintaining the scandalous primacy of a woman! But though in the Fourth Gospel Mary is the first to *see* the risen Lord, she is not, as we have just noted, the first to *believe*. Mary revisits the tomb, where she sees two angels, who ask why she is weeping; she explains that she is looking for Jesus' body. Turning from the tomb she sees Jesus himself, but fails to recognize him, even when he asks the same question; she therefore gives the same explanation, and it is only when he speaks her name that she recognizes him. As with the story of the beloved disciple, the story of Mary suggests that seeing Jesus is not in itself important: certainly it is not this that convinces her of the truth, for it is not seeing Jesus or even hearing his voice that persuades Mary that he has been raised. Nor is touching him important, for she is instructed not to cling to him: the moment of recognition comes when Jesus addresses her by name. We recall Jesus' description of himself as the good shepherd, who calls his own sheep by name (John 10.3) – the good shepherd who lays down his life for his sheep and who takes it up again (10.11, 17–18); this good shepherd knows his own sheep, and they know him (10.14), so that when they hear his voice, they follow him (10.27). Mary, hearing Jesus call her by name, recognizes him.

Mary's 'confession' of Jesus here stands alongside the affirmations of faith made by other women earlier in the Gospel. In John 4.29, the Samaritan woman raised the suggestion that he might be the Messiah, and through her witness – however hesitating – many of her fellow-countrymen came to confess him as Saviour of the world (vv. 39–42). In that passage, John remarks on the extraordinary fact that Jesus engaged in conversation with a woman (v. 27). Later, in conversation with another woman (Martha), Jesus leads her to confess him as 'the Messiah, the Son of God, the one coming into the world' (John 11.27). Elsewhere, of course, similar statements have been found in the mouths of men – John the Baptist (1.29, 34), Nathanael (1.49) and Peter (6.69); we will find another attributed to Thomas in 20.28. What is noteworthy is that *any* of these confessions should be attributed to women. Now Mary addressed Jesus as 'Rabbouni' – Aramaic for 'my teacher'. Compared with the words attributed to the Samaritan woman and to Martha, this appears to be far less significant; nevertheless, her role is just as important. Martha confessed her faith in Jesus when he said 'I am the resurrection and the life' (11.25). Now, Mary Magdalene confessed her faith in Jesus as the Risen One. The word 'Rabbouni' is the recognition that Jesus is indeed alive, and serves to identify the figure whom Mary meets in the garden with the 'rabbi' whom we have met in the previous chapters, about whom we have already learned so much. The person whom she took to be a gardener is none other than Jesus, who is 'the Lord' (v. 18).

Did the fourth evangelist think of Mary as attempting to take hold of Jesus' feet, as the women are said to have done in Matthew 28.9? Certainly he tells us that Jesus instructed her not to cling to him (v. 17). These words have caused some commentators great difficulties, partly because of the apparent contradiction with what Jesus says to Thomas in 20.27, partly because of the explanation that Jesus gives to Mary – 'I have not yet ascended to the Father':[6] how can Jesus be touched *after* his ascension, but not *before*? However, this explanation may well provide the clue to the words' meaning. Mary, recognizing Jesus as the master whom she loves, and addressing him by a familiar term, perhaps imagines that he has been restored to life in the way that Lazarus was (11.44), and that all will continue as it did before. But she has to learn that things will never be the same again. The new, permanent, relationship with Jesus depends on him returning to the Father. When he addresses Mary, Jesus has not yet ascended to the Father (v. 17); it would seem that Mary alone is privileged to see him in this interim period before he returns to the one whom he goes on to refer to as 'my Father and your Father, my God and your God' – the one to whom he is still obedient. Jesus' words remind us of two passages earlier in the Gospel which referred to the Son of man ascending into heaven.[7] They also pick up an idea that was constantly emphasized in the Johannine Farewell Discourses (John

14—17), where we were told that Jesus was about to go to the Father who had sent him.[8]

As in Matthew, Jesus entrusts Mary with a message for the disciples. This message, however, is not about seeing him in Galilee, but an announcement of his coming ascension. There is no promise here that the disciples will in fact see him: rather, the message refers only to the fact that Jesus is leaving them to go to the Father. The evangelist tells us that Mary delivered the message to the disciples. Although that message contained no promise of a future appearance, the disciples were perhaps meant to remember Jesus' promises that he would come back to them (14.3, 18, 28) and that they would see him again (16.16–22). Certainly, that same evening, Jesus is said to have appeared to ten of the disciples, and this time, seeing apparently *is* important, for Jesus shows them his hands and his side. But this is not where the emphasis of the story lies, for this meeting, like the final scene in Matthew, is basically a commissioning: Jesus hands over responsibility to the disciples with the words 'As the Father has sent me, so I send you.' He breathes on them, saying 'Receive the Holy Spirit.' The words of John the Baptist, back in 1.33, revealing Jesus to be the one who baptizes with the Holy Spirit, have at last been fulfilled. So, too, have Jesus' own promises about providing the Holy Spirit to be 'another Advocate'.[9] Jesus also gives the disciples the power to forgive and to retain sins – another reminder of the Baptist's words, since it was he who identified Jesus as 'the Lamb of God, who takes away the sin of the world' (1.29). Now Jesus, who has died as the true passover lamb,[10] gives his disciples the power to forgive or to retain sins. With these two echoes of the

Baptist's witness to Jesus, which opened John's narrative, we have already an *inclusio*, reminding us of the beginning of the Gospel.

But there is more to come! In the third of these Jerusalem-based stories, we have an account of how Jesus appeared to the eleven – this time, apparently, in response to Thomas's *unbelief*, since Thomas, demanding far more in the way of proof than had been given to the other disciples, had insisted that he would not believe unless he saw and touched Jesus. This is not what we expect! In contrast to Mark, who insists that we shall not see the risen Lord unless we believe and obey, John portrays Jesus appearing to one who has declared his unbelief in order to persuade him! Nevertheless, he uses the story to make the same point, for in the event Thomas apparently did not need to touch Jesus to be persuaded, and the evangelist ends with Jesus' remark that though Thomas has believed because he has seen him, the truly blessed are those who do *not* see him, yet believe. It would seem that John, like Mark, is after all trying to persuade his readers that resurrection appearances are not important. The climax of this last scene is Thomas's confession of Jesus as his Lord and his God, and with that recognition of him as 'God' we are taken back with a jolt not just to the beginning of the narrative but to the opening declaration of the Gospel: 'the Word was God'. What the evangelist is doing reminds us of one of those sets of Russian dolls – one *inclusio* fitting snugly inside another.[11] This one invites the reader to echo Thomas's words and say: 'Yes, now I comprehend that this is what this whole story means.'

To Thomas, the supreme doubter, then, is given the

honour of making the most profound pronouncement in the whole Gospel. His confession, together with Jesus' response, pronouncing those who believe without seeing to be blessed, form a fitting climax to the book. The evangelist rounds it off with the comment that Jesus did many other signs which he has not recorded, as though to remind us that his story is incomplete; but in *this* Gospel, the story is incomplete because it is impossible to write about *everything that has already been done by Jesus*, rather than about *what is still to come*. What the evangelist *has* selected has been written so that his readers may believe that Jesus is the Messiah, the Son of God.

As in the other Gospels, we have not only an echo of its opening lines, but a reminder of what the whole story has been about, here evoked quite brilliantly in that one word 'signs'; for throughout the Gospel, Jesus has performed various signs which have pointed to the truth of who he is; and now the author spells out what he believes that truth to be. And like the other evangelists he looks forward too. The disciples have been commissioned by Jesus to continue the work that he has begun,[12] and John's final words are a direct appeal to his readers for faith in Jesus: once again, the story cannot be completed unless we join in. His purpose in writing is, he says, to persuade us that Jesus is the Messiah, the Son of God, and so find life in his name. The book may have come to a tidy end, but John does not expect us to put the book back on our shelves with a sigh of satisfaction and the thought that this was a good story: this is meant to be the kind of book that changes lives.

But, in fact, that is *not* the end of John's Gospel. Although the author rounded things off neatly, someone apparently could not leave well alone, for in chapter 21 we are given another ending. The matter is, of course, extremely complex: was this epilogue written by the original author, or was it the work of a redactor? Unlike the two endings which were added to Mark's Gospel, this chapter is similar in style and theology to the rest of the book, and is thus an integral part of its final form. Many commentators believe that the Gospel has gone through a long process of redaction, and if they are right, then this is only one editorial addition among many. Whatever the explanation, it is part of the Gospel as we have it now, and whoever wrote it may well have written other parts of the book also. Certainly it is written in typically Johannine style; it even contains a sign – the huge catch of fish – together with the customary discourse related to the sign, which here takes the form of a conversation between Jesus and Peter. The sign – which takes place when the disciples obey Jesus' instruction to cast the net on the other side of the boat – is an implicit command to catch 'fish'; the conversation a direct command to tend 'sheep'. The metaphors may seem mixed, but the messages conveyed by both sign and conversation are linked: Jesus commissions his disciples to make still more disciples, and he entrusts to Peter the task of caring for them. The story of the miraculous catch repeats in picture language the command Jesus gave to the disciples in John 20.21: 'As the Father has sent me, so I send you.' They are to gather men and women into the community of believers. Peter, restored and forgiven, is to continue the work of Jesus; like the Good Shepherd, he too will lay down his life for the sheep, and his death, like that of Jesus, will glorify God.[13]

This final scene is set, not in Jerusalem, but in Galilee. The Fourth Gospel thus combines the tradition found in Mark and Matthew, that Jesus was seen in Galilee, with Luke's version of the story, which places his appearances in Jerusalem. It was appropriate that Mark and Matthew should relate the Galilee tradition, since they both understand Jesus' ministry to have been based in Galilee. Luke, though he tells the same story, begins both his Gospel and his second volume in Jerusalem, and it is fitting that the Gospel should end there. In the Fourth Gospel, however, Jesus' ministry is divided between Galilee and Jerusalem, and it is perhaps not surprising that the redactor thought that the accounts of resurrection appearances in Jerusalem should be balanced by an appearance in Galilee, where Jesus' first 'sign' (pointing forward to his glorification) was performed (2.1–11).[14]

The story contains various interesting features. First, we notice that, as with the appearance to Mary, the disciples do not at first recognize Jesus. It is only when they obey his instructions that the beloved disciple realizes that it is the Lord who is standing on the shore. So once again, as in *Mark's* final words, 'seeing' Jesus depends on having sufficient faith to obey his command. Even then, it is only the disciple who is closest to Jesus who recognizes him. Impulsive as ever, it is Peter who jumps into the sea to go to Jesus (v. 7), just as he had rushed first into the tomb (20.6).

The central scene in this chapter is a meal, to which the disciples are invited to bring their fish, only to find that cooked fish and bread are already provided. The implications are clearly eucharistic: it is the risen Lord who is the host, not the disciples. And though the disciples do not dare to ask him who he is, they know that it is the Lord (v. 12): as in Luke's story of the travellers to Emmaus, there is no mistaking the identity of the one who presides at this meal. This story, then, points beyond itself to the belief that Jesus is present in the eucharistic meal, when Christians gather together in his name. But it points backwards, too, for though John does not record the institution of the Lord's Supper as do the other evangelists and Paul,[15] he does relate the story of how Jesus fed the crowds with bread and fish (John 6). That miracle was interpreted by John as a sign of Jesus' true identity and the significance of his death and resurrection. No wonder, then, that the disciples are said to have recognized him as he gave them bread and fish! The meal is also a foretaste of what is still to come – the messianic banquet – whose super-abundance is perhaps hinted at in the bumper catch of fish.[16]

The disciples were instructed how to catch fish. Like the saying in Mark 1.17, we may assume that this is to be interpreted as a command to evangelize. The careful record of the number of fish – 153 – indicates that this is significant, though it is not clear why! Perhaps the fact that it is a 'triangular number' – that is, it is the sum of the numbers between 1 and 17, which when represented by dots on consecutive lines make an equilateral triangle – is important; moreover, 17 is not only itself a prime number, but it is the sum of 10 and 7, each of which was regarded as representing completeness. Are they, then, to evangelize *all* the nations?

The final scene in this chapter, like the first, is primarily a commissioning: Peter is commissioned to tend Jesus' lambs.

But first he needs to be forgiven. Here is perhaps one explanation as to why a redactor might have thought it necessary to continue the story, for so far Peter, who denied that he was a disciple,[17] has not been restored; now he is called once again to follow Jesus, and to continue his work. Jesus asks him three times whether he loves him: Peter is hurt by this, but it is necessary, since his threefold denial needs to be undone (13.36–8; 18.15–18, 25–7). The significance of the conversation between Jesus and Peter is clear. Each time, Jesus addresses Peter as 'Simon'; by his threefold denial he has shown that he is not yet rock-like, so the name 'Cephas' (i.e. 'Peter', 1.42) is inappropriate. But though Simon Peter failed in the past to lay down his life for Jesus (13.37), he will do so in the future.

The final sign and Jesus' words to Peter show very clearly that the story John is telling has still not come to its end: and now it is not simply because the evangelist has been unable to write down everything that Jesus did, but because there are still disciples to be made, and still members of the flock to be cared for. When *will* it end? Presumably when Jesus returns, since in response to Peter's question about what will happen to the 'other disciple' whom Jesus loved, Jesus hints that he may perhaps remain until then. But perhaps he will not! The evangelist may well have included this brief exchange between Jesus and Peter in order to deal with a problem – possibly one caused by the recent death of the beloved disciple. Had not Jesus said that this disciple would remain until he himself returned? John's answer is 'No: Jesus said only "*If* such a thing were to happen, what business is that of yours?"' Peter's task is to tend the sheep (vv. 15, 16, 17), and he can do this only if he is prepared to follow Jesus (v. 19) – the very thing that the beloved disciple is already doing, without any special prompting. Following Jesus will mean, for Peter, that he will die as a martyr; like Jesus, he will glorify God by his death. What the beloved disciple will be called on to do is not Peter's concern.

In a final note, the redactor tells us that it was the beloved disciple who 'bears witness to these things' and who 'wrote them'. 'These things' may well refer to chapters 1–20. Whoever wrote this last chapter identified the beloved disciple as the source of the tradition contained in the Gospel, and added 'and we know that his testimony is true'. Who are the 'we'? Does the word refer to the final redactor of the Gospel and others who assisted him? Or does it refer to the whole believing community, who are thus drawn into the narrative? If *we* know that his testimony is true, then action is clearly demanded of us. But *how* do we know that his testimony is true? No reason is given, but presumably it is because the one to whom he bears witness is the true light (1.9), through whom truth and grace are fully revealed to the world (1.17). Once again, the language reminds us of John's Prologue.

Who was it added this last chapter to the Gospel? Was he responsible for other sections of it also? And why did he think the addition was necessary? Was it just to rehabilitate Peter? Was it because he had heard these stories from other Christians, and wished to incorporate them into the book? Was it because he felt the need to include a command to the disciples to evangelize the nations? Or did he perhaps decide that the original ending of the Gospel had not been sufficiently open-ended, and that the Christian community had to be reminded that they had a task to do?[18] Certainly the significance of Jesus' commission to the disciples is underlined in these final lines.

There is something else odd about John's ending; whereas in Mark, the risen Christ never made an appearance, in John he never departs.[19] Even with this second attempt, Jesus never actually takes leave of the disciples, as he does in Matthew and Luke. Is this because the fourth evangelist almost identifies 'resurrection' with 'ascension'? – 'almost', because of course he does imply that the ascension took place after Jesus was seen by Mary Magdalene.[20] Is the fact that Jesus never takes leave of the disciples the Johannine equivalent of the promise made in Matthew 28.20 that 'I am with you, to the end of time'? Certainly the author's final words, declaring that 'if every one of the things that Jesus did were written down . . . the world itself could not contain all the books that would be written' seem to be intended to remind us that *his* story is inevitably incomplete. Nothing could be more open-ended than this![21] These final words echo what was said in 20.30, though this time the reason for not attempting to write everything has been expressed in an exaggerated way. The words strike us as absurd hyperbole, but hyperbole was an accepted literary convention in the ancient world. Similar in meaning to this final sentence is the comment attributed to Rabbi Johann ben Zakkai:[22]

If all the heavens were sheets of paper, and all the trees were pens for writing, and all the seas were ink, that would not suffice to write down the wisdom that I have received from my teachers; and yet I have taken no more from the wisdom of the sages than a fly does when it dips into the sea and bears away a tiny drop.

Hyperbole or not, John's comment is intended to point us to the impossibility of summing up the glory revealed in Christ. The first-century Jewish philosopher Philo wrote in similar terms:[23]

> Were [God] to choose to display His own riches, even the entire earth with the sea turned into dry land would not contain them.

The final sentence of John 21 has seemed to some to be a weak conclusion, amounting to little more than an excuse for not writing any more, but it is surely an acknowledgement of the greatness of the subject, and the impossibility of doing it justice: if the universe cannot contain the books that might be written about Jesus, that is because he is the 'Word', through whom all things were made (1.3), and who has made known to us the nature of God himself (1.18). This being so, 'the entire earth with the sea turned into dry land would not contain' the account of what he did during his ministry, in which he revealed the riches of the glory of God. If there is so much more to learn about Jesus than has been written in John's Gospel, then the reader's voyage of discovery has only just begun.

6

Epilogue

...To make an end is to make a beginning.

The end is where we start from.

(T.S. Eliot, *Four Quartets*, Little Gidding V)

One might perhaps have expected that the way in which the evangelists brought their books to an end would be far removed from the way in which they began. In fact, as we have seen, this is not so. In many respects, 'endings' perform the same function as 'beginnings', pointing to the significance of the story that is being told. Taken together, we find that the beginning and end of each of our narratives form a neat *inclusio*, so that the final words of each book invite us to look back to the beginning of the story and to start reading it once more, with new insights into its meaning.

In none of these books, however, does the *inclusio* give us closure. On the contrary, our 'endings' all look forward to what comes next. All five of the books we have looked at have what we have termed 'suspended endings'. Like some modern playwrights, each of our authors invites the members of his audience to take up the story and write the final scene of the drama for themselves. In their closing pages, in very different ways, each of them reminds us of the story that has been told, and each of them takes us back to the beginning of that story; but each is anxious to remind us, his readers, that the narrative is not yet at an end, and that it is up to us to continue it.

The endings of our five books, like their beginnings, are carefully crafted and appropriate to their authors' purposes; each of them is clearly 'made to measure', not picked up off a supermarket shelf. Yet each in its own way conveys the same message: the story that has been told is the work of God, and its continuation depends on those to whom it is entrusted. In their various endings, each of our writers urges us to turn the end into a beginning, and to continue writing the story for ourselves.

Perhaps what we have discovered in looking at the Gospels and at Acts is simply a phenomenon of a great deal of literature; or perhaps the conviction shared by these authors that they had been caught up into the ongoing story of God's salvation for the world was what led them to adopt this particular literary form. Precisely *because* this story is ongoing, it *cannot* have closure, for that will come only at the End of all things. All our synoptic evangelists remind us that 'the End is still to come'.[1] The time of restoration is still in the future (Acts 1.6–7). The Christian community lives in the time *before* the End, the time between the resurrection of Christ and the resurrection of believers: in the meantime, Jesus is with them until the end of the age (Matt. 28.20). Only in the Fourth Gospel is this emphasis on a future 'End' missing: for John, it would seem that Jesus' exaltation on the cross is the end of the story. He tells us that Jesus loved his disciples 'to the end',[2] and that with his death, all things are completed.[3] In John, the tension between present and future has become a tension between below and above,[4] and between earth and heaven.[5] The evangelist stresses the *present* relationship between Christ and the believer rather than the need to watch and wait for the End. 'No longer imminent, the End is immanent.'[6] Yet even in John, there is an expectation of a future Parousia (21.23); and even in John, the story is incomplete unless the disciples obey and cast their nets where they are commanded (21.4–11), unless Peter tends the sheep (21.15–17), and unless the readers respond and believe (20.31).

The stories in the Gospels' endings are all concerned with Jesus' resurrection.[7] There are interesting similarities and striking differences between these stories, and even within one Gospel they sometimes appear to be contradictory: Jesus appears and disappears, yet he is no ghost, for he eats fish;[8] he must not be touched, and yet invites Thomas to touch him.[9] These stories represent different aspects of the believing community's conviction that Jesus was alive, different ways in which they had experienced his presence after the resurrection. Since it is these stories that provide the endings to our Gospels, we should perhaps not be surprised that these endings all prove to be 'suspended'. For it may be that the ending which is in fact a new beginning is the inevitable way to express a gospel which is about death and resurrection. To the disciples, what seemed like an ending proved to be the beginning of a new life.

This conviction that death is not the end because Jesus has been raised is one which many have since shared, believing that for them, too, death would be followed by life. Perhaps no-one has experienced it more poignantly or expressed it more powerfully than Dietrich Bonhoeffer, whose last recorded words on the eve of his execution in April 1945 may provide a fitting ending to *this* book:[10]

This is the end – for me, the beginning of life.

Notes

Preface

1. I had already explored the topic of Beginnings in a book on the Prologues of the Gospels: Morna D. Hooker, *Beginnings: Keys that Open the Gospels*, London: SCM Press 1997; Harrisburg, Pa.: TPI 1998.

1. Beginnings and Endings

1. He is quoted by various ancient writers, e.g. P. Porphyry, *Quaestiones Homericae*, Iliad XIV 200: ξυνὸν γὰρ ἀρχὴ και πέρας ἐπὶ κύκλου περιφερείας .
2. Elsewhere in the New Testament, we find that Paul's letters, following the literary conventions of his day, normally begin with an indication of the themes he is going to discuss, and often conclude with a brief summary alluding to them. e.g. Rom. 1.1–7 and 16.25–7; Gal. 1.3–5 and 6.11–16; 1 Thess. 1.2–10 and 5.23–4. Revelation begins and ends with the announcement by John, witness to the visions recorded in the book, that the Lord, who is Alpha and Omega, is coming (Rev. 1.1–8; 22.8–21).
3. Morna D. Hooker, *Beginnings: Keys that Open the Gospels*, London: SCM Press 1997; Harrisburg, Pa.: TPI 1998.
4. R.A. Burridge, *What are the Gospels? A Comparison with Graeco-Roman Biography*, SNTS Monograph series 70, Cambridge: Cambridge University Press 1992.
5. See, for example, Xenophon, *Agesilaus*; Plutarch, *Lives*; Tacitus, *Agricola*; Suetonius, *Lives of the Caesars*. The exception is Philostratus' Life of Apollonius of Tyana, but this was written in

the early third century AD, and may to some extent have been modelled on the Gospels.

6. The use of 'suspended endings' in ancient literature is discussed by J. Lee Magness, *Sense and Absence*, SBL Semeia Studies, Atlanta: Scholars Press 1986.

7. 1 Samuel ends with the death of Saul, and 2 Samuel continues the story with David's lament over Saul and Jonathan. 2 Samuel then tells the story of David's reign, but we are not told of his death until the opening chapter of 1 Kings. That book ends with the death of Ahaziah, which is then described at greater length at the beginning of 2 Kings.

8. Although placed before 1–2 Chronicles in the Hebrew Bible, Ezra–Nehemiah continue the story and bring it to a conclusion. Once again, these two books are really one, and appear as such in the Septuagint.

9. Because the evangelists proclaim the fulfilment of Old Testament hopes, they have sometimes been said to be maintaining a 'realized' eschatology, in contrast to the 'futuristic' eschatology of the prophets. It is better, however, to describe their outlook as an expression of 'inaugurated' eschatology: what has happened in Jesus is the beginning of what *will* happen in the future.

2. Mark's Ending: Lost or Suspended?

1. The first appears in many English translations immediately after Mark 16.8. The second is Mark 16.9–20.

2. A. Farrer, *A Study in St Mark*, Westminster: Dacre 1951, p. 178.

3. The suggestion that Mark intended to end at 16.8 was first made by Julius Wellhausen, in 1903 (*Das Evangelium Marci*, Berlin: de Gruyter). Twenty years earlier, Westcott and Hort had dismissed such a possibility as absurd: 'It is incredible that the evangelists deliberately concluded either a paragraph with ἐφοβοῦντο γάρ, or the Gospel with a petty detail of a secondary event, leaving his narrative hanging in the air' (Brooke Foss Westcott and Fenton John Anthony Hort, *The New Testament in the Original Greek*, vol. 2, Introduction and Appendix, Cambridge and London: Macmillan 1881, p. 46).

4. See J. Lee Magness, *Sense and Absence*, SBL Semeia Studies, Atlanta: Scholars Press 1986.

5. *Poetics* 7. 3.
6. Cf. also the abrupt ending of Virgil's *Aeneid*.
7. This view was first expressed by Aristophanes and Aristarchus. See Denys Page, *The Homeric Odyssey*, Oxford: Clarendon 1955, pp. 101–36; G.S. Kirk, *The Songs of Homer*, Cambridge: Cambridge University Press 1962, pp. 248–51.
8. Several examples were cited by R.H. Lightfoot, in his *Locality and Doctrine in the Gospels*, London: Hodder & Stoughton 1938, pp. 10–15. Other examples have been found since, e.g. Menander's *Dyscolos*, lines 437–8; Plotinus, *Ennead* 5. 5; Cicero, *Ad Allicum* 12. 12. 2. The examples refer to sentences, sometimes sections, ending in *gar*, not books, though 'if a sentence or paragraph can end with γάρ, a book can too' (P.W. van der Horst, 'Can a Book End with γάρ? A Note on Mark xvi.8', *JTS* NS 23 (1972), pp. 121–4).
9. A few mss. follow the Hebrew more closely, and add 'at his presence'.
10. This verb, used in 9.15 of the disciples' reaction to Jesus when he returned to them after the Transfiguration, and of Jesus himself in the Garden of Gethsemane, expresses strong human emotion.
11. See also Mark 4.41; 5.15.
12. Throughout the Gospel, men and women were afraid (*phobeomai*) when they were confronted with Jesus' extraordinary power (Mark 4.41; 5.15, 33, 36; 6.50); his disciples had been afraid when he spoke of future suffering and death (Mark 9.32; 10.32); his enemies were afraid of him because they did not understand him (Mark 11.18, 32; 12.12). Frequently this fear is linked with lack of faith or understanding (Mark 4.40; 5.17, 36; 6.52; 9.6 (with *ekphobos*), 32; 11.18, 32; 12.12.
13. Mark 5.25–34; 7.24–30. They have also been commended for their devotion (12.41–4; 14.3–9). They are said to have served Jesus (1.31; 15.41; cf. 10.45). Like the Twelve, they followed Jesus in Galilee and went to Jerusalem with him (15.40–1), but seem to have found it easier than the Twelve did to respond to the demands Jesus made of his disciples.
14. Cf. R.H. Lightfoot, *The Gospel Message of St. Mark*, Oxford: Oxford University Press 1950, p. 93: 'to the fact of the resurrection St. Mark has given full expression in 16.1–8'.
15. The second Mary is described here as 'the mother of James the

younger and of Joses'.

16. The western text reads 'James'; other mss. read 'James and Joses'.

17. The verb is *diakoneō*, which is used also in Mark 10.45 of service by the Son of man. Elsewhere it is used only at 1.13 and 31.

18. Cf. Andrew T. Lincoln, 'The Promise and the Failure: Mark 16.7, 8', *JBL* 108 (1989), pp. 283–300 (p. 288), reprinted in William R. Telford (ed.), *The Interpretation of Mark*, 2nd edn, Edinburgh: T. & T. Clark 1995, pp. 229–51 (p. 233).

19. See U. Wilckens, *Resurrection*, Eng. trans., Edinburgh: Saint Andrew Press 1977, pp. 34–5; Reginald H. Fuller, *The Formation of the Resurrection Narratives*, London: SPCK 1972, p. 64.

20. See 1.34; 3.12; 5.43; 7.36; 8.26, 30.

21. Thomas E. Boomershine and Gilbert L. Bartholomew, 'The Narrative Technique of Mark 16.8', *JBL* 100 (1981), pp. 213–23, argue that Mark's use of a simple, brief sentence at the end of his story is a stylistic technique which is intended to 'bring about maximum stress' (p. 220).

22. T.J. Weeden's suggestion that Mark intends us to understand that 'the disciples never received the angel's message, thus never met the resurrected Lord', is contrary to all the evidence. The traditions reported by Paul in 1 Cor. 15.1–7 would have been widely known, and Mark could hardly have ignored them. See Theodore J. Weeden, *Mark: Traditions in Conflict*, Philadelphia: Fortress 1971, p. 50.

23. Cf. Norman R. Petersen, 'When is the End not the End? Literary Reflections on the Ending of Mark's Narrative', *Interpretation* 34 (1980), pp. 151–66: 'the reader is compelled by the narrator to respond' (p. 153).

24. Frank Kermode's comment on the novel which fails to gratify our expectations because it departs from what we expect is apposite: 'The reader is not offered easy satisfaction, but a challenge to creative co-operation' (*The Sense of an Ending*, New York: Oxford University Press 1967, p. 19).

25. In chapter 1, we have quotations from scripture and the witness of the Baptist; when Jesus appears on the scene we know that he is the one whom scripture and John have spoken about. In chapter 16, we have the empty tomb and the witness of the young man; we are asked, once again, to 'put 2 and 2 together',

even though this time Jesus does not appear.

26. See e.g. C.F. Evans, 'I Will Go Before You Into Galilee', *JTS* NS 5 (1954), pp. 3–18.
27. See Ernst Lohmeyer, *Das Evangelium des Markus*, 17th edn, Göttingen: Vandenhoeck & Ruprecht 1967, *in loc.*
28. See W. Marxsen, *Mark the Evangelist*, Eng. trans., Nashville and New York: Abingdon 1969, p. 85.
29. This is how Marxsen explains the message.
30. Cf. Zech. 14.4–5.
31. For Mark, *hodos* means not simply 'road' but 'way' – the way of the Lord (1.23; 12.14), the way Jesus took to Jerusalem (9.33–4; 10.17, 32, 46; 11.8), and hence the way of discipleship (10.52; cf. Acts 9.2; 18.25–6; 19.9, 23; 22.4; 24.14, 22).
32. See Mark 4.13, 40; 7.18; 8.14–21; 9.19. Cf. also 6.52; 10.32–45.
33. Cf. Lincoln, 'The Promise and the Failure'.
34. The Latin ms. k.
35. Mark ends at 16.8 in both ℵ (Codex Sinaiticus) and B (Codex Vaticanus).
36. W.R. Farmer, *The Last Twelve Verses of Mark*, Cambridge: Cambridge University Press 1974, attempts to argue that the ending is original, but fails to explain these differences.
37. Cf. John 20.11–18.
38. Cf. Luke 24.13–33.
39. Cf. Luke 24.36–43.
40. Cf. Matt. 28.19–20.
41. Cf. Mark 8.11–13.
42. Cf. Luke 24.50–1; Acts 1.9.

3. Matthew's Ending: The Great Commission

1. According to W.D. Davies and Dale C. Allison, Jr, *A Critical and Exegetical Commentary on the Gospel according to Saint Matthew*, 3 vols., Edinburgh: T. & T. Clark 1988–97, Matthew's ending 'is, from the literary point of view, perfect, in the sense that it satisfyingly completes the Gospel' (vol. 3, p. 687). Although, as we shall see, it does 'complete' the Gospel by using *inclusio*, we have some sympathy with the view of Bernard Shaw (which Davies and Allison say they 'fail to under-

stand', n. 56), 'that Matthew's "narrative abruptly stops" and "has no ending"'. It would seem that Shaw was pointing out the feature which they themselves acknowledge when they describe 28.16–20 as 'an open-ended ending' (vol. 3, p. 686).

2. I am assuming here the priority of Mark, since I am convinced that the evidence overwhelmingly supports this: the issue makes little difference, however, to most of my discussion of how the evangelists have handled the tradition.

3. Somewhat puzzlingly, Matthew associates the *earlier* earthquake with the resurrection of 'many saints'. As if aware of the difficulty this creates, however, he adds that they emerged from the tombs and were seen only *after* Jesus' resurrection.

4. Unless, that is, the phrase 'everything that had happened' in v. 11 is meant to include the angel's words to the women.

5. Although Matthew attributes this to Jeremiah, he quotes Zech. 11.12–13; Jeremiah refers to a potter in 18.1–11 and to buying a field in 32.6–15.

6. Exod. 3.12; 19.17, 20.

7. The Greek reads simply *hoi de*, which normally means 'but they'. The construction normally introduces a change of subject, and so might refer to someone *other* than the disciples; but since no-one besides the eleven has been mentioned in this passage, this rules out the translation 'but others'. Translators normally conclude that the construction has been used in a partitive sense, but a clause beginning in this way would normally follow a clause introduced by *hoi men*, the two together giving the meaning 'Some . . . but others . . .'.

8. Matt. 8.26; 14.31; 16.8.

9. There is considerable debate as to whether or not Matthew believed that the teaching that the disciples were instructed to teach the Gentiles included obedience to the Law. Would he have opposed Paul's view that Gentiles were not required to be circumcised and keep the regulations of the Law (cf. G. Barth, in Günther Bornkamm, Gerhard Barth and Heinz Joachim Held, *Tradition and Interpretation in Matthew*, Eng. trans., London: SCM Press 1963, pp. 62–75, 131–7, 159–64), insisting that the commandments must still be kept, or agreed with him that Christ had fulfilled the requirements of the Law? Matt. 5.17–20 insists that every jot and tittle of the Law must be observed. But

perhaps 'all is accomplished' or fulfilled (v. 18) refers to what takes place in Jesus (cf. 1.22; 21.4; 26.56)? In 25.31–46, 'all nations' are judged by their behaviour to the poor and needy, and not by any adherence to particular commandments: this behaviour is love for God and for one's neighbour, which is the true content of the Law (22.34–40). Matthew makes no reference to any need for the circumcision of Gentiles – only their baptism. Cf. M. Bockmuehl, *Jewish Law in Gentile Churches*, Edinburgh: T. & T. Clark 2000, p. 163: 'In the end, Jesus' teaching and interpretation of the Law is the highest authority; and this alone is what the Apostles are to teach the new, Gentile community of his disciples.'

10. The phrase is literally 'the end of the age'; when this age ends, so will time.
11. Matt. 25.31–46; 26.64.
12. Matt. 7.29; 9.6; 10.1; 21.23–7.
13. See Davies and Allison, *Matthew*, vol. 3, p. 683.
14. Matt. 16.21; 17.9, 12, 22–3; 20.18–19.
15. Matt. 26.64; cf. 16.27; 24.30–1.
16. Jesus' teaching in Matthew 5—7 concerns behaviour. His instructions to the disciples in chapter 10 concern what they should *do* – and what they may expect, as a result.
17. Cf. Matt. 7.21–3; 25.31–46.
18. See Matt. 13.39–40, 49; 24.3.
19. Matt. 4.14–16; 12.17–21; cf. Isa. 9.1–2; 42.1–4.
20. There is an obvious tension between these passages and sayings such as 10.5 and 15.24. Jesus appears to have concentrated his ministry on his own people. Although Gentiles were also responding to his message (8.5–13; 15.21–8), they were exceptions to the rule. But this does not mean that the Gentiles are excluded from the Kingdom. Israel's task is to be a light to the Gentiles, but her people cannot undertake this until they themselves repent.
21. Commentators disagree as to whether Matthew understands Jesus to be 'God', or thinks of him as the one in whom the divine favour and blessing are manifested. See Davies and Allison, *Matthew*, vol. 1, p. 217.
22. See Exod. 3.14; Isa. 43.10; Job 9.8; Ps. 77.19–20.
23. In Matt. 11.25–7, Jesus spoke of the intimate relationship

between the Father and the Son.

24. Exod. 2.1–10. In Matthew, the slaughter is Herod's reaction to the information of the wise men that a king has been born; for a parallel to this, see Josephus, *Antiquities* 2. 9. 2 (205–9). Josephus goes on to describe how Moses' father is warned by God in a dream, and how his mother conceals him, 2. 9. 3–4 (210–23).

25. These verses have been aptly described as the '*grand finale*' of the Gospel. See G.N. Stanton, *A Gospel for a New People: Studies in Matthew*, Edinburgh: T. & T. Clark 1992, p. 345, n. 2.

26. See Davies and Allison, *Matthew*, vol. 3, pp. 679–70.

27. David Catchpole, *Resurrection People: Studies in the Resurrection Narratives of the Gospels*, London: Darton, Longman & Todd 2000, p. 52.

28. Davies and Allison comment that only Josh. 1.1–9 and Jer. 1.1–10 have the following four elements (found also in Matt. 28.16–20): 'πορεύομαι, repetitive πᾶς, the instruction to do what has been commanded (with ἐντέλλομαι), and the promise of divine presence (with μετά)' (*Matthew*, vol. 3, p. 679). In fact, these elements are found in Exod. 3.1—4.17/7.1–2: *poreuomai*, 3.11, 18, 19; *entellomai*, 7.2; the promise of the divine presence, 3.12; 4.12; *pas* is found once only, in 7.2, but Jer. 1.1–10 also has only one. Moreover, Jer. 1.1–10 is generally thought to be influenced by Exod. 7.2; cf. Robert P. Carroll, *Jeremiah*, Old Testament Library, London: SCM Press 1986, p. 99. Matthew's phrase *panta hosa eneteilamēn humin* appears to echo *panta hosa soi entellomai* in Exod. 7.2.

29. There is another account of Moses' call, in addition to that in Exod. 3.1—4.17, in 6.2—7.7.

30. Dale C. Allison, in his book *The New Moses: A Matthean Typology*, Edinburgh: T. & T. Clark 1993, does not make this point. Is this why, surprisingly, he fails to notice the parallels between Matthew 28 and Exodus 3? See pp. 262–6.

31. *Exodus Rabbah (Yithro)* 27.9; *Mekhilta Bahodesh* 5; *Sifre Deuteronomy* 343.

32. Many of the features in Exodus 3—4 echoed in Matthew 28 are found also in the account of Moses' return to the mountain in Exodus 33—4.

33. *Mishnah Aboth* 3.2.
34. Davies and Allison, *Matthew*, vol. 3, p. 688.
35. *Poetics* 7. 3.

4. Luke's Loose Ends

1. Hans Conzelmann, *The Theology of Saint Luke*, London: Faber; New York: Harper 1960, Eng. trans. of *Die Mitte Der Zeit*, 2nd edn, Beiträge zur historischen Theologie 17, Tübingen: Mohr 1957.
2. See Stephen Farris, *The Hymns of Luke's Infancy Narratives: Their Origin, Meaning and Significance*, JSNT Supplement series 9, Sheffield: JSOT 1985.
3. Luke 1.32–3, 54–5, 68–79; 2.11, 30–2, 38.
4. Luke 2.32; cf. 4.24–7.
5. Cf. Acts 1.3 with 8.12 and 28.31.
6. Cf. Acts 2.22 with 2.43, 8.13 and 14.3.
7. Cf. Acts 5.17–41; 7.54–60; 16.19–34.
8. T.S. Eliot, *The Cultivation of Christmas Trees*.
9. Acts 1.1–2. See Loveday C.A. Alexander, 'The Preface to Acts and the Historians', in Ben Witherington III (ed.), *History, Literature and Society in the Book of Acts*, Cambridge: Cambridge University Press 1996, pp. 73–103.
10. This particular understanding of God's activity in history is often termed 'Salvation history'.
11. For example in the early chapters of the Gospel, as we have noted, Luke not only uses Old Testament language, but appears to have the story of the birth of Samuel in mind in relating the birth of John the Baptist (see 1 Sam. 1.11—2.11). If C.F. Evans's theory is correct, he used Deuteronomy as the outline for the 'travel narrative' in 9.51 to 18.14. See 'The Central Section of St Luke's Gospel', in D.E. Nineham (ed.), *Studies in the Gospels: Essays in Memory of R.H. Lightfoot*, Oxford: Blackwell 1957, pp. 37–53.
12. This verse is missing in the mss. of the Western text, which means that it may be a later addition.
13. It is no accident that it is at this point that recognition comes; they are reminded of past occasions when they have seen him break bread. The action points us back to the meals which Jesus

has taken with his disciples in the Gospel, and forward to the meals which the Christian community will share in Acts.

14. For the importance of these twin themes, see M.D. Hooker, 'Beginning from Moses and from All the Prophets', in Marinus C. De Boer (ed.), *From Jesus to John: Essays on Jesus and New Testament Christology in Honour of Marinus de Jonge*, JSNT Supplement series 84, Sheffield: JSOT Press 1993, pp. 216–30.

15. They are instructed to proclaim in his name repentance leading to forgiveness of sins. This, too, is said to be part of what is written, Luke 24.46f. The story of Acts, like that of the Gospel, is thus seen to be the fulfilment of scripture, and part of the continuing activity of God.

16. The reference to Jesus being carried up to heaven is probably a later addition, as is the statement that the disciples worshipped him.

17. Luke 1.14; 2.10.

18. Luke 1.64; 2.28.

19. Luke 2.37.

20. Luke 2.11; cf. 1.43.

21. Luke 2.32; see also 4.24–7.

22. The exception to this is the story of the centurion's slave, told in Luke 7.1–10 – though it lacks the final sayings found in Matthew's version (Matt. 8.5–13). Nor does Luke include other references to Gentiles found in Matthew, such as Matt. 2.1–12; 4.15–16; 12.18–21; 28.19. The most remarkable 'omission' is the story of the Gentile mother told in Matt. 15.21–8//Mark 7.24–30.

23. Luke 3.16. The promise is found in the mouth of John the Baptist, whose witness can be assumed to be reliable, since he has been declared to be Jesus' forerunner, and to be himself filled with the Holy Spirit, by Gabriel: Luke 1.13–20.

24. On the ending of Luke, see R. Tannehill, *The Narrative Unity of Luke–Acts*, vol. 1, Philadelphia: Fortress 1986, pp. 277–301.

25. On the parallels between Luke 24 and Acts 1, see Mikeal C. Parsons, *The Departure of Jesus in Luke–Acts: The Ascension Narratives in Context*, JSNT Supplement series 21, Sheffield: JSOT Press 1987.

26. The phrase may be an allusion to Isa. 49.6, which is quoted in Acts 13.47.

27. Cf. Luke 1.32–3, 54–5, 68–79; 2.11, 30–2, 38.
28. Paul, like Jesus, is said to be innocent of the charges brought against him, and has been delivered into the hands of the Romans (Acts 28.17) by the Jews, who have plotted against him.
29. P. Schubert, 'The Final Cycle of Speeches in the Book of Acts', *JBL* 87 (1968), pp. 1–16, says of this passage that it 'summarizes the context of chapters 22–26 very aptly' (p. 10).
30. For a brief account of these, see C.K. Barrett, *A Critical and Exegetical Commentary on the Acts of the Apostles*, vol. 2, Edinburgh; T. & T. Clark 1998, pp. 1248–50.
31. Cf. Luke 21.20–4.
32. See Acts 20.25, 38; 21.11, echoing the passion prediction in Luke 18.32. Since other predictions are fulfilled, we can be sure that this one will be too.
33. See previous note.
34. See P.R. Davies, 'The Ending of Acts', *Expository Times* 94 (1982–3), pp. 334f.
35. Cf. Acts 26.6.
36. H.J. Cadbury, *The Making of Luke–Acts*, London: SPCK 1958, p. 324; cf. F.F. Bruce, *The Acts of the Apostles*, London: Tyndale Press 1952, p. 481, who describes the ending as 'artistic and powerful'. See also J.H. Moulton and G. Milligan, *The Vocabulary of the Greek Testament*, London: Hodder & Stoughton 1930, p. 20.
37. Paul's final journey to Rome and arrival there are depicted as something of a triumph. On the voyage to Rome, he was shipwrecked on Malta, but the whole ship's company survived and Paul himself was given a hero's welcome on the island. On the outskirts of Rome, he was met and welcomed by the Christian community.
38. Acts 19.21; 23.11.
39. Cf. 26.6–7, where this hope is linked with hope for resurrection (v. 8). In 23.6, Paul is said to be on trial 'concerning hope in the resurrection of the dead'; cf. 24.15, 21. This future hope is, of course, understood by Luke to be based on the resurrection of Jesus: 17.31; 26.23.
40. Cf. what is said about the disciples whom Jesus meets on the way to Emmaus; their eyes have not yet been opened (Luke

24.16, 31); they are slow of heart to believe (24.25).

41. Luke 24.21; Acts 1.6; cf. Luke 1.32–3.
42. See Acts 23.6; 24.15; 26.6–7. Cf. the reference to David's hope in Peter's speech, 2.26–7.
43. Acts 23.6; 26.6–7.
44. The Jewish rejection of Jesus is a theme which unites the beginnings and ends of both Luke and Acts. It is symbolized in Luke 4.21–30, acted out in the passion story, recalled in Acts 2.22–36 and repeated in Acts 28.23–8.
45. Acts 13.44–9; 18.5f.; 28.23–9. Cf. also 19.8–10.
46. Acts 9.15; 20.21. Luke regularly depicts Paul as beginning his mission in a city in the synagogue – even after the scenes in chapters 13 and 18.
47. Cf. J. Jervell, *The Unknown Paul: Essays on Luke–Acts and Early Christian History*, Minneapolis: Augsburg 1984, p. 16: 'Christianity is for Luke the religion of Israel.'
48. Cf. a similar comment in the parallel passages: 13.43 and 18.8.
49. The verse is found in many late manuscripts, and appears to be an addition.
50. The failure of the Jews to respond is thus presented in a positive light, as providing an opportunity for the Gentiles to hear the gospel. See also B.J. Koet, *Five Studies on Interpretation of Scripture in Luke–Acts*, Leuven: University Press/Peeters 1989, pp. 119–39.
51. On the ending of Acts, see Tannehill, *The Narrative Unity of Luke–Acts*, vol. 2, pp. 330–43; Wm. F. Brosend II, 'The Means of Absent Ends', in Ben Witherington III (ed.), *History, Literature and Society in the Book of Acts*, Cambridge: Cambridge University Press 1996, pp. 348–62.
52. Schubert, 'Speeches', describes Acts as ending on an 'optimistic note' (p. 10).
53. Some commentators assume that Luke thinks that the proclamation of the gospel in Rome means that it has been taken 'to the ends of the earth'. But the parallelism in Isa. 49.6 implies that it is to be taken to *all* the nations, and this has not yet taken place.
54. Cf. also the book of Numbers, which ends with the people camped on the wrong side of the River Jordan.
55. Cf. H.J. Cadbury, *The Making of Luke–Acts*, London: SPCK

1958, p. 323, 'We may be again arguing from our own tastes rather than from the author's own conception of his task.'

56. Daniel Marguerat, 'The End of Acts (28.16–31) and the Rhetoric of Silence', in Stanley E. Porter and Thomas H. Olbricht (eds), *Rhetoric and the New Testament: Essays from the 1992 Heidelberg Conference*, JSNT Supplement series 90, Sheffield: JSOT Press 1993, pp. 74–89, compares Herodotus, as well as Homer and Virgil.

57. *Homilies on Acts* (1) 55 (Migne, *Patrologia Graeca*, LX, coll. (15) 382).

5. John's Endings and Beginnings

1. These are the first and the last words of 'East Coker'. They are based on the motto of Mary, Queen of Scots: *En ma fin est mon commencement.*

2. John 3.14; 8.28; 12.32, 34 (*hupsoō*).

3. John 7.39; 12.16, 23; 13.31–2; 17.1, 4–5 (*doxazō*).

4. John 14.18–19; 16.16.

5. The readers of the Gospel are presumably numbered among those who believe without seeing. Paradoxically, it is the beloved disciple, who 'saw and believed', who is the paradigm for those who do *not* see and yet who believe: unlike Thomas, the beloved disciple was prepared to believe without seeing the risen Christ.

6. For an account of some of the bizarre explanations that have been given, and of various attempts to evade the problem by amending the text, see Raymond E. Brown, *The Gospel According to John*, vol. 2: *XIII–XXI*, Anchor Bible, New York: Doubleday 1970, pp. 992–3.

7. John 3.13; 6.62.

8. John 14.12, 28; 16.5, 10, 17, 28; 17.13.

9. John 14.16–17, 26; 15.26; 16.7–15.

10. John puts the death of Jesus at the time when the passover lambs were being killed. See John 18.28.

11. It is worth noting an even earlier 'closure', which occurs as early as 12.44–50. This passage concludes the first part of the Gospel, which is then followed by the Farewell Discourses (chs. 13–17) and Passion Narrative (chs. 18–20). Commentators often note

the echoes of earlier teaching in this passage (notably v. 47, which picks up what is said in 3.17), as well as the fact that these verses are in turn echoed in the teaching in chapters 13—17. Perhaps more significant, however, are the links between 12.44-6 and 1.1–18: to believe in Jesus is to believe in God (cf. 1.12); those who see Jesus see the one who sent him (cf. 1.14, 18); Jesus is the light coming into the world (cf. 1.9); darkness cannot prevail in his presence (cf. 1.5). In vv. 48-9 the word spoken by Jesus will judge men and women on the last day, because what Jesus says and does has been given to him by the Father. This is hardly surprising to those who know that the word which Jesus speaks is spoken by the one who is himself the Word (1.1), and who in speaking both reveals his own glory – the glory which he has as an only Son from the Father (1.14) – and makes the Father known (1.18). The link with John 1.1–18 is noted by Graham Stanton, *The Gospels and Jesus*, 2nd edn, Oxford: Oxford University Press 2002, p. 113.

12. The language is typically Johannine: 'As the Father sent me, so I send you', John 20.21.

13. John 21.19. Cf. 13.31-2; 17.1.

14. In the early chapters of his Gospel, John appears at times to have deliberately 'paired' stories based in Galilee and Jerusalem: each pair of stories is concerned with a similar theme. Cf. 2.1–11 with 2.13-23; 4.46-54 with 5.1–18; chapter 6 with chapter 7.

15. Matt. 26.26-9; Mark 14.22-5; Luke 22.14-21; 1 Cor. 11.23-6.

16. The significance of the meal, in the present, past and future, is summed up by Paul in 1 Cor. 11.26: 'As often as you eat the bread and drink the cup, you proclaim the Lord's death till he comes.'

17. John 18.15-18, 25-7.

18. The closing verses of this chapter repeat the statement in 20.30 that there was much more that could have been told, and affirm that the testimony of the author (or source of the tradition) is true.

19. His ascension is foretold by Jesus in John 20.17; are we to assume that it has happened by the time we come to 20.27?

20. John 20.17. In the same sort of way, as we have already seen, he coalesced Jesus' crucifixion with his exaltation; see above, notes 2 and 3.

21. Cf. the final verses added to Ecclesiastes by an editor, who comments on the many proverbs taught by the Teacher, and remarks: 'Of the making of books there is no end' (Eccl. 12.9,12). Although just as open-ended as John's final verse, this typically cynical approach produces a very different effect.
22. B. Talmud *Sopherim* 16.8. Rabbi Johann taught in the first century AD, but the Talmud was written much later.
23. *De post. Caini* 144.

6. Epilogue

1. Matt. 24.6//Mark 13.7//Luke 21.9.
2. John 13.1. This is the only use of the noun *telos* in the Fourth Gospel.
3. John 19.28, 30, where the cognate verb *teleō*, 'to end' or 'to complete', is used. Another cognate verb, *teleioō*, with similar meanings, is used of Jesus completing the work given to him by his Father in John 4.34; 5.36 and 17.4; of what happens through him in 17.23; and of the fulfilment of scripture in him in 19.28.
4. John 3.3, 7, 31.
5. John 1.32; 3.27, 31; 6.31–58.
6. Frank Kermode, *The Sense of an Ending*, New York: Oxford University Press 1967, p.25.
7. This theme, as we noted above, p. 63, is also present in the closing verses of Acts.
8. Luke 24.30–1, 36–43.
9. John 20.17, 27.
10. The words were part of a message to George Bell, Bishop of Chichester. See *Letters and Papers from Prison*, ed. E. Bethge, London: SCM Press 1953, p. 181.

For Further Reading

Stephen Barton and Graham Stanton (eds), *Resurrection: Essays in Honour of Leslie Houlden*, London: SPCK 1994

David Catchpole, *Resurrection People: Studies in the Resurrection Narratives of the Gospels*, London: Darton, Longman & Todd 2000

Reginald H. Fuller, *The Formation of the Resurrection Narratives*, London: SPCK 1972

Frank Kermode, *The Sense of an Ending*, New York: Oxford University Press 1967

R.H. Lightfoot, *Locality and Doctrine in the Gospels*, London: Hodder & Stoughton 1938

——*The Gospel Message of St. Mark*, Oxford: Oxford University Press 1950

J. Lee Magness, *Sense and Absence*, SBL Semeia Studies, Atlanta: Scholars Press 1986

Norman Perrin, *The Resurrection Narratives: A New Approach*, London: SCM Press 1977

Ulrich Wilckens, *Resurrection*, Eng. trans., Edinburgh: St Andrew Press 1977

Rowan Williams, *Resurrection*, London: Darton, Longman & Todd 1982; rev. edn 2002

Index of Modern Authors

Index of Modern Authors